Hot Chocolate For The Mind
By Dwayne Perkins

D1540297

Dwayne Perkins

First ebook Edition: December 2012

Dedication

To the memory of Gloria Lewis and Otis Perkins.

Author's Note

About eight years ago I had the notion to write a book. I didn't know what and I didn't know how. So I started a blog. I looked at it as a way to connect with fans of my stand-up comedy while working on my writing until the time came to pen my book. I quickly learned that writing was very freeing compared to stand-up comedy. Although the feedback is not as immediate neither is the need to be "laugh out loud" funny. There's no urgency to adhere to a certain amount of laughs per minute. When I'm writing, there's no two drink minimum, no hecklers, no ordering of drinks and most importantly no bills being settled. The connection with the reader can be as potent if not stronger than the one with the live audience. I still love performing though and I encourage any reader to see me live.

About 5 years ago I also had the notion to write a manifesto. I know there are many doctrines that do a bang up job of giving people life guidelines. People seem to either not know or not listen to those doctrines so I thought maybe just maybe I could reach people. Propose a concise new set of words to live by that would be easier to understand.   Of course, anything I could write in my manifesto would merely be paraphrasing what most religious books already say. I also had to remind myself that many men of late who have done horrible acts also wrote manifestos. Maybe they were already inclined to do evil acts before they penned their manifestos but the thought that the act itself of writing a manifesto drives people crazy gave me pause.

In the end I realized that while writing my blogs, I was writing my first book and a manifesto of sorts.   My life tenets hinted at in every story told and I didn't have to become a menace to get my point across. The title is an obvious play on a title of very popular books but it's also based on feedback I've received. I'm told these collection of blogs have a uplifting effect. You need not look for inspiration though. If you find it, great. Above all, I seek to bring you quality laughs. Feel free to read straight thru or skip around. By the way QSN = Quick Side Note. It'll pop up a few times in this book. Thanks for buying my first book. Enjoy.

Www.dwayneperkins.com
Twitter.com/funnydp

CITY OF ANGELS

I'm Becoming A Stripper

My apologies for the sensational title. While the title is technically true, there won't be ravenous cheering women flinging money at me any time soon. At least not in a public. I'm going to dig out an extra power outlet strip and start bringing it with me to coffee shops. I sometimes go under the moniker of "Facilitator of A Good Time." I think facilitating electric harmony is equally important.

There's always an appreciative sigh of relief when someone produces a power strip. Bringing an end to the game of musical power outlets that naturally takes place at coffee shops; especially those in the greater Los Angeles area. I want to be the source of that ahhhh. Some people want to build low-income housing or feed the poor. I want to prevent hipsters from losing their data. If America's next great screenplay isn't on my laptop at least I can provide electricity for the laptop that it is on. Of course I run the risk of powering up the machine that brings the world the next greatly lame reality show.

The daytime coffee shop is a sea of individuals gathered but often not connected. Things like chess and power strips builds community. So I think it's fair to say I'm becoming a community activist. Right? I am a man of the people and my new plan is an extremely minor way to "stick it to the man." I'm sure the bean counters at your favorite coffee shop have calculated their costs based on the number of outlets they have in the store. They probably didn't account for a power supply Robin Hood taking power from the rich and giving it to the ironic.

I will limit my electric siphoning when I'm in mom and pop establishments. And please if you're on my power strip, no solitaire. I strip for workers.

It Sometimes Rains in Southern California

Los Angeles, after a rain fall is one of the prettiest sights I've seen. Everything is so crisp and clear. You can see for miles and all the colors are sharp and bright; the palm trees, mountains, buildings all in Glorious Technicolor*. You can actually see things you never noticed, like a building right off the highway you drive on everyday. I get sad on these post rain days because I remember this life size postcard is brought to me by the rain washing away all the smog that usually clouds the LA skyline. The smog Angelinos breathe in daily. Then I think of all that smog being washed into the land and sea. Then of how just one day later the view will be back to its normal hazy state and how I won't see that building tomorrow. Then I pump up Lily Allen's "LDN" and try to forget the whole thing.

*http://en.wikipedia.org/wiki/
Technicolor

Rumble In The Garden

So, I recently got a Thai massage. I had sworn off Thai massages because I usually feel like I lost an MMA* fight afterward. People assure me that that's a good thing. No pain no gain, release the tension...yada...yada. But how can going into a place feeling pretty good and leaving with a limp and hunched over be a good thing?

Luckily, the lady gave me an option on the beat down. I never knew there were grades to the Thai massage. I thought, you go in, get kneed in your back for an hour, pay $40 and go sleep it off. But she gave me the hard, medium or soft options. I opted for medium. I was tempted to go with soft. I guess I couldn't help but feel I wasn't getting my money's worth if there was entirely no suffering. Some pain, some gain.

This ended up being the most therapeutic Thai massage I've ever had.

Of the hour session, 40 minutes were quite enjoyable. The first 20 minutes were quite stressful though as I had a bit of vapor that wanted out. Is it still flatulence before it's released? I'm pro choice on flatulence. Not all flatulence need make it to the world. Plus, I didn't want to be that guy. Surely if you rip one, you're looking at a $20 dollar tip… minimum. Funny thing is…I got a strange feeling that she knew my condition and was rooting for the vapor. I was on a collision course with a staunch right to flatulencer. She started hitting me in the back, pounding on my legs. It felt like I had come there just to get help letting one go. Like that was the service they provided. Like she would stop after I released and say "All done!". But I was determined to not be the butt of the salon's jokes for the next month. It all came to a head when she did the machine gun chops to my back and immediately followed that up with twisting my torso while putting me in a full nelson.** And just like that my body sent the air pocket to some holding area where it comfortably stayed until well after my massage. I looked embarrassment in the face and came out victorious. I relaxed and enjoyed the rest of the massage. I think the masseuse noticed my tension exhale and reluctantly accepted that I would not be the story of the week and went back to non flatulence inducing techniques.

The toughest part of the 20 minute flatulence standoff was the muzak playing in the background. The cheesiest hit pop records of all time all done with traditional Asian instruments. It was like being stuck in an elevator in a bamboo garden. That muzak really took me out of my mental game. It was only after my body suppressed the threat for good that I was able to enjoy the silliness of Lionel Ritchie's Hello, done on a Guzheng*** with waterfall sounds in the background.

I tipped her 10 dollars at the end for a job well done but I couldn't help but feel that maybe she should have tipped me.

*MMA Mixed Martial Arts.

http://www.mixedmartialarts.com/

** Full Nelson: Wrestling grip where you wrap your hand around the neck in head. Very hard to escape once the grip has been applied http://en.wikipedia.org/wiki/Image:Farmerburnsfigure24fullnelson.jpg.

*** Guzheng one of many Traditional Chinese instruments http://www.philmultic.com/home/instruments/

http://en.wikipedia.org/wiki/Guzheng

Hustle and Go

I was sitting outside of a Coffee Bean and Tea Leaf in the Korea Town section of Los Angeles enjoying a beverage with a friend. A disheveled gentleman came up to me and said he was conducting a survey. And by disheveled I mean a Hot Mess. I thought to myself, really, and what organization sanctioned this "survey". But I had a little time to see where this was going. So I motioned for him to continue. He cleared his throat and said...

Hot Mess: Hi!

So I said...

ME: Hi.

He then pulled out a napkin, unfolded it, produced a pencil, and wrote down a number. He then, put the pencil away, refolded the napkin and put it back in his pocket. Oh, so that was the <u>official</u>

napkin? He said only 6 people had said hi back to him out of 23 "surveyed." Just when I thought maybe this was a guy who just wanted to share his crazy without asking for money, Hot Mess informed me that the survey process did have some overhead and to continue his research he would need some funding. Having already been sufficiently amused, I gladly gave him some change.

I think either my face or the tone of my voice must be truth serum or maybe the truth came after I gave Hot Mess my donation. After successfully tallying my results, Hot Mess says to me...

HOT MESS: Which way is Sunset? Do you think I could hustle more money there or here?

Et tu Hot Mess? You were hustling me?

But I was one of the people who said hi! I told him to proceed to Highland and Hollywood to get his hustle on. I also gave him directions to get there. I wonder if Hot Mess needs an agent.

Someone Framed Me

This might seem like my 99th blog about the 99 cents store but I assure you it's probably only my fifth. With that said I was recently in my own personal Disneyland and came across a poster frame for...drum roll please...99 cents...duh. Not a bad deal for a pretty decent picture frame. But here's where it gets all Twilight Zoney.

The guy in the stock picture already in the frame looks like a spitting image of a younger me. And this is ME saying this. I actually had to study the picture for a half hour to be absolutely certain it wasn't me. He even had on a shirt that smacks of my '96 threads. I was finally able to conclusively say it's not me based on two things: 1st, No apparent gap in his smile. Mind you it's a profile pic so it's hard to see what kind of gap, if any, he was working with. But you can airbrush out a gap or airbrush in some pearly whites. But the 2nd and more solid tell-tale was this guy's ears.

He has a weird thing going on with his lobes. I pride myself on having stellar lobes. Mike Tyson salivates at the mere mention of me. But still, he looks like me enough that I might just hang the poster as is.

Now, I only have to come up with back stories for the other models in the picture.

Oh that's Gary, he became a roadie for a Hootie and the Blowfish cover band just days after this picture was taken.

Oh and that's Brenda, we kinda had a thing but we never saw eye to eye on what the thermostat should be set on. That girl froze me out...She ended up marrying an actuary who liked wearing sweaters all the time. But as fate would have it he got transferred to Phoenix. He was willing to give up sweaters but she wasn't willing to give up 65 degree temps. She says they argue about the electric bill but besides that they're happy.

I will also have to explain why my photo of me and my friends says $5.95 in the corner. (I told you the 99 cents store was a good deal!)

Clean Up On Aisle Six

So I was recently in a Rite Aide in Hollywood California. While spanning the aisles for travel sized lotion bottles and floss I spied a girl getting ready in the beauty aisle. She was full on dolling up for the night right there in Rite Aid. Is it shoplifting if you only use one application and you don't even take the bottle out of the store?

I've long been a proponent of taking a squirt of lotion for the road. I wouldn't scream bloody murder if I bought a bottle of lotion with 2 squirts missing. But this girl was using their mirror and various hair products with impunity. All she needed was a lawn chair from the household section and she could have set up a full Salon right there on aisle 6.

How was she getting away with it? The Rite Aid on Fairfax and Sunset has bigger fish to fry than coming down on a person making the hair product aisle her personal medicine cabinet. They have to deal with panhandlers blocking the entrance, people sleeping in nooks and crannies in the store, shoplifters taking entire boxes from the store room and crazed sugar junkies screaming for ice cream.*

Miss primp actually went about her business with reckless calm. I can't imagine she could have been any more comfortable at home than she was there under the Rite Aid fluorescents with muzack playing.

A few days later and I'm still not sure if I think she's one righteous dudette or a menace to society. I respect her hustle but can't help thinking that her total disregard for rules may be a bad thing for either society or those close to her.

But it squarely proves one of my longstanding theories. Act like you belong and people won't bother you. Besides the lack of precedence her commitment to acting like nothing was

wrong probably kept the Rite Aid
workers at bay.

*Rite aid sells fresh ice cream. Really
good for 1.29 a scoop. You say
Coldstones and I say Rite Aid…Let's call
the whole thing off…

And I would've Gotten Away with it...

So I'm in one of my Los Angeles coffee shops I'm known to frequent. I was in the mood for a pastry but the "day olds"* were gone except for the chocolate chip croissants and nothing from the fresh pastry offerings tickled my fancy.

QSN: I went on record back in '01 saying that chocolate chips are put into way too many things. You can check my voting record. I went against the popular vote and said "NO" to putting chocolate chips into bagels. Sadly, I was out voted.

So, with pastries out of the question, I naturally shifted my attention toward biscuit type products to accompany my Jasmine tea (Biscotti and such). One of the counter–top crunchy items on display was a thing the coffee shop called a Frankie Snack. It seemed to match my snack criteria, small and inexpensive. I was a little thrown by the ingredients but I've eaten worse.

It wasn't until I went to the register to check out that the barista informed me that what I had in my hand was actually a doggie biscuit. I was seconds away from eating a Scooby Snack, with no mystery or mystery van anywhere in sight. The barista said people make that mistake all the time. You think? Do they sell apple fritters at the check out counter at Pet World? Maybe the label should read "DOG FOOD" in bold letters. Or at least call it a Scooby Snack. What if I had taken a bite as I waited in line? Did I mention these doggie biscuits were self serve? I did think it was odd that chicken stock was one of the ingredients. I made note of that but somehow I was still on board (Damn, I really will eat anything). We give dogs our left over tater tots. Would it kill us if we ate some of their biscuits?

America can we mistake dog food for human food....Yes We Can.

* day olds – pastries from the day before. You take a hit on freshness but they're usually only a buck or less.

Break Away

I was in the Dollar Tree in Reseda, CA last week. Everything in the store costs a dollar. Think of it as an upscale 99 cents store. There was a cashier standing at a closed register. When people came up to her register, she told them she was on a break. Does this woman know the meaning of break? It's only a break if you leave your place of work... or at least leave your work station. A break with out a change of location is not a break at all... it's a breather. She willingly, albeit unknowingly, downgraded her break to a mere breather. It's like a person in in a halfway house who doesn't leave. Game and match point, purpose defeated.

Not to mention she's a cashier. And her standing there only serves as a big tease. Strippers don't sit on the stage and read a magazine. Some jobs require you to be out of sight if you're not available for service. A doctor can't hang out in the ER playing Tetris while someone walks in with a javelin in their neck. Now that's what I call adding insult to injury. (hee hee)

DOCTOR: That looks painful. I'll be done here pretty soon. After I take down the high score and eat a jelly donut, I'll stop that squirting from your jugular.

NECK SQUIRTER: Sure doc, take your time. Isn't it ironic that you taking a breather is preventing me from breathing… I can't feel my feet.

Fine, standing in line a few extra minutes with Shasta and a 9 volt battery is not as bad as a javelin to the neck, but I still don't want to see unavailable cashiers right in front of me. My Shasta's getting warm!

Women are from Venus

Some kids were riding scooters on my block in Los Angeles. Three boys went zooming by me with two girls bringing up the rear. I would say the ages ranged from seven to ten. As the girls passed me, I heard one say to the other, "Let's stop riding so we can go and talk." And I heard the other girl say, "Okay." And there you have it, folks. In a nutshell, all you need to know about the difference between women and men. On a perfect sunny day with nothing to do but be a kid, run around, and have fun, these girls opted to abandon all that fun and sit and talk. The boys had nothing on their minds but squeezing in as much activity as possible before they had to call it a day. Flash ahead twenty years and those boys are going to be at such a loss when they get into a debate with those girls. The boys won't even know the girls have had a twenty year head start.

Baby Powder Run

I was at a Ninety Nine cents store in Los Angeles last week. The guy ahead of me in line had only one item: a big bottle of Johnson & Johnson's baby powder. The total was $1.07 after taxes. This guy rifled through the fanny pack he was wearing for change. His quest for one dollar and seven cents in loose change took about 3 minutes with almost half of the cost paid in pennies. I'm pretty sure he snuck in some Canadian coins in as well. Finally, the guy reaches a buck o-seven and the eight people waiting in line all exhale a sigh of relief. The cashier put his baby powder in a bag. Then, our baby powder purchaser demanded a receipt. He asked for a receipt with attitude as if the cashier was trying to pull one over on him. I thought putting the baby powder in a bag was a more dignified act than the purchase called for.

Our baby powder bandit then put his

baby powder in a knapsack, threw it over both shoulders and walked to the parking lot where his bike was locked to a newspaper stand. He unlocked his bike and rode off with baby powder in tow.

I had to tell the whole story because it begs so many questions:

If you're down to your last dollar, should you be spending that dollar on baby powder? Why the backpack? Why the bike? Why the fanny pack? Why even leave the house to buy baby powder (especially when you have to ride a bike there)?

Or to use a Jerry Seinfeld convention... if you're down to your last dollar, I don't think chafing is your biggest problem.

Maybe in the end, for some, chafing is much worse than hunger.

Home is Where the Heart's is

Shout out to Heart's, my local breakfast spot. It was the classic look that first got my attention, well that and the $3.99 pancake, egg, sausage & bacon combo. I said to myself...
ME: "self, you got to try HAUGHTS!"(modified for my NY accent)

I took heed to my own advice and went inside and I've been going there for 3 years now. It's straight out of the seventies. It looks so much like a diner that it almost seems fake. Like something constructed for filming purposes but not really serviceable. It's serviceable my friends. They make the bomb pancakes and French toast. They even have killer dinner specials. You can eat like Kobayashi* for under 10 bucks. I'm talking bread, soup, entrée and dessert all under 10 bucks. The place is actually run by a Chinese family. So here's the kicker...you can also get Chinese food. You can sit across from a friend eating pancakes while you down some Egg Foo Young. Choices people, that's what America is all about.

But if you go to Hearts make sure you get a beverage, coffee, tea or juice. There's a notable dip in service and friendliness if you don't.
SERVER: Coffee, tea, juice?
ME: No thank you.
SERVER: No?! There's your menu on the

floor...I'll be back never

Maybe their profit margin is too low to take the hit of people eating without having a beverage? Or maybe the otherwise friendly owners used to own a Comedy Club and just can't get the notion of a two drink minimum out of their systems. Still a thumbs up though. Great job Hearts! Cash Only btw.

* famous competitive eater. Pioneered the "dipping hot dogs in water before you eat them" style of overeating.

http://en.wikipedia.org/wiki/ Takeru_Kobayashi

Pawn of the Dead

I recently went into a pawn shop. I was toying with the idea of picking up an electric guitar. Yes, I play (acoustic). Yes, I suck. No, I won't ever play for you. Despite my suck–a–tude, I've wanted an electric guitar for a long time now. Why not get a good deal on a second hand one right? Well, because pawn shops are evil. You could cut through the despair with a knife. These items weren't donated out of the kindness of peoples' hearts. Quiet to the contrary, it felt like most of the items on the shelves came in via broken hearts and spirits. Every ring, tv, watch came with a tale of lost hope, lost direction and even lost humanity. The items still carried those tales. The negative energy was palpable. Even my breathing became labored. (in all fairness though, that could have been the Drakkar No 5. the proprietor apparently sweats from his pores.)

I didn't want any part of that energy. I'll just buy Guitar Center's base model from some tight jean wearing teenager who's in a garage thrash band and can barely hide his disdain that I'm a poser buying a lame guitar. Patronizing, I can take but I couldn't see myself benefiting from the plight of these sad strangers. Plus, what if I pick the one guitar that's haunted with its past owner's soul? The guitar would wreak havoc on me and my family. It would take us a while to figure out that the guitar is pitting us against each other. We would, of course, bury the guitar deep in the Mojave dessert, to end the terror once and for all, only to find it sitting in the living room all clean, shiny and menacing when we got back home. Somebody get M. Knight Shyamalan on the phone.

Seriously though, that pawn shop made me almost as sad as Wal-Mart does.* I think the sadness is amplified by the fact that the past owners harbor hopes of coming back one day and reclaiming their stuff. Good luck with that.

*Wal-Mart can be depressing but I must confess that I love Wal-Mart anytime after midnight and before 8am. I usually find myself in Wal-Mart late night in some random town after a show. Fun times.

I Love Technology...

... as much as the next guy. I even had a Commodore 64 back in the day. Dating myself big time. But maybe I had a Commodore 64 computer instead of building blocks... Okay, fine, I didn't, but at least I didn't have a Eniac as a kid. Of course, that would have been bigger than the apartment I grew up in. I figure the people reading this who have to Google Commodore 64 can also Google Eniac while they're at it.

While I do love and embrace technology, I can't believe how quickly we've all become dependent on it for the most menial of tasks. I called my friend on her cell phone in Target just to see what aisle she was in. People went shopping together for hundreds of years without cell phones. It's not like every year, millions of families went to Sears, split up and lost touch forever.

Guy 1: Jeff, whatever happened to your mom?
Guy 2: I lost her in the great linen sale of '78. But thank God the Jeffersons found me in aisle six and raised me as one of their own.

Here's how people managed way back before cell phones... they shouted a name. The other person responded and they moved toward the sound of their respective voices until... eureka.

I took a picture, using my Treo phone, of myself in the 99 cents store just to see how I looked in one of the hats they had for sale. Did I really need a visual aid to figure out a hat from the 99 cents store would probably look like crap. I basically used a four hundred dollar portable computer to help me decide if I could blow a buck on a hat. Of course this ebook is made possible by technology and the acceptance and usage of said technology. So in the end I…

…still love technology… always and forever

http://en.wikipedia.org/wiki/ENIAC

http://en.wikipedia.org/wiki/Commodore_64

Keep on Moving

I was recently cruising down the 405 in beautiful Los Angeles...rewind...Ok, I was recently in bumper to bumper traffic on the 405 with my windows up to reduce my intake of the LA Smog I was currently contributing to. I was perusing through my preset radio stations searching for the perfect song to take my mind off my potentially frustrating stagnant state. The batteries in my radio transmitter that plays my mp3 player on an empty radio station were dead. So I was at the mercy of my factory installed 6 preset radio sans CD player, satellite radio or even cassette player for that matter.

Now, I don't hit a good song and stop. I'm too optimistic/hard to please to have my in-car radio strategy be that simple. I go through all the presets and sample what's being played. Only after ensuring I know the best song currently playing (with at least a minute of play time left of course) then and only then do I settle in to the best song available and get my groove on.

This can be frustrating to passengers in the car with me but luckily on this day I was alone and in rare preset jump around mode. Then, I came across Soul to Soul's "Back To Life" and from the beginning at that.
However do you want me....However do you need me...

This song was the perfect ailment to my traffic woes. But you have to play by your own rules, right? What was I to do? Could I really do better that Soul to Soul at this very moment? After, letting the intro play (I'm not a masochist) I decided to let it ride and change the station. I mean it was possible that "Midnight train to Georgia", "Let's Get It On", "Ain't No Stopping Us Now" or maybe even some MJ might be playing.

With a press of my index finger I

jumped to another preset only to hear Soul to Soul's other smash hit, "Keep on Moving", blaring, also from the beginning. I was in a can't lose and can't win situation all at once. Either way I would jam out with a bonafide crazy joint* and miss out on a song that was bananas.

In the end I went with "Keep On Moving"...yellow is the color of sunrays.

My system's not perfect.

*Crazy Joint – a really good song. Usually one that makes you want to move.

Noisy Flat

A while back I was in my bathroom and I let one rip. Unfortunately, the walls in my bathroom are thin. I can hear the elderly couple that lives next to me banter and sometimes bicker.

Imagine the horror that pulsed through my body when I heard the husband say to the wife, "Did you fart?" Which the wife of course vehemently denied then counter accused the husband of farting. This went back and forth without either one budging. I could have settled their argument by flushing my toilet. Their trust in each other would have been restored but then they would know it was me, their next door neighbor that let one go. I stayed there, as I was, for over 15 minutes. They'll just have to go to a marriage counselor because I wasn't about let Edith and Archie in on my bathroom business.

I was basically held hostage in my

bathroom by my own noisy flatulence. At least it wasn't a silent yet deadly one. A man should be able to "express" himself in his own bathroom. Wouldn't you know, the one time I don't blare Jack FM from my bathroom radio during a "session" and I get called out like that. There's no way Ma & Pa hear my vapor if I had Thin Lizzy blasting. I could have simply timed my releases to the baseline of "The Boys Are Back in Town."

I take nothing for granted now and I turn on my bathroom radio when I brush my teeth or blow my nose or smooth out my eyebrows.

Hamlet, Two People

I recently went to see Hamlet2. I think the "2" represents the total number of people in the theater...including me. I sat in the middle of the theater as to get the best viewing angle and best catch the surround sound. The other guy sat in the corner of the last row. This should have served as a hint of what I was in for. I mean who, given an empty theater chooses to sit in the corner like a refugee? A guy with absolutely no self control, that's who. I actually spent ½ of the movie looking back trying to figure out if there was a committee back there because I couldn't believe one guy could make that much noise. This guy was having full on conservations with himself but that wasn't as scary as the dialogue he had with the movie screen. At one point he shouted to the screen:

CRAZY DUDE: I didn't get that one!

It seemed like he was waiting for an

answer. For a split second I considered explaining the joke to him, the least I could do for my lone viewing partner. But instead I let one of the other voices in his head field the question. This guy was walking a tight rope of sanity. It's hard to enjoy a comedy while you're terrified. The real problem was that the one man gang was behind me. I'm sure he was harmless but I wasn't in the mood for my thoughts to become famous last words.

ME: I thought to myself he's loud and a bit odd but he's okay...then I woke up in the hospital... How did the movie end?

"2", also represents the number of options I had. Either deal with the voices behind me or sit in the last row with him to keep him in my sights. Damn! Why are crazy people so strategic?! To be fair to him though, he was there before me and maybe looking forward to a solo viewing. Perhaps they should install a viewing room in his asylum.

I give kudos to Hamlet 2. I laughed my ass off even with danger looming behind me. As for the other guy?...I think they enjoyed it too.

SHORTIES

Pretty Sneaky Sis

I spent most of last weekend playing Connect 4 with my 10 and 9 year old little cousins. There's no better confidence builder than pouncing on little kids. When the smoke cleared, my win-loss record was 57-2. The two losses? Well, one was dumb luck and the other should have an asterisk because my cousin put in 2 red pieces at a time. I called it cheating. She called it improvising. Well, she would have called it that if she knew that word. I rule.

Hush Little Baby

I'm afraid to hold small infants, but not for the usual reasons. I saw on TV that perceived beauty is mainly related to facial symmetry and that even infants prefer faces that are symmetrical and pretty. So I don't hold babies because I don't want to be judged by a three month old.

"Now, there there, baby…. please stop crying. I changed you, fed you, you're well rested. Are you saying I'm ugly? Well, you won't be three months old forever, and one day you're gonna have to hold a baby. And then we'll see how symmetrical your face is!"

Multitasking Gone Horribly Wrong

Yesterday, while driving on Olympic Blvd in Los Angeles, I saw a man of at least eighty driving a big old-person-mobile and brushing his teeth while he drove. His head barely cleared the dashboard and he was using one hand to drive and the other to control tartar build-up. First off, I give kudos to him for still having his real teeth. Perhaps his unhealthy obsession with dental hygiene is the reason he's still working with his original pearly whites. And I won't even entertain the thought that he was brushing dentures while they were in his mouth, while he drove a full size death-mobile. I'm scared of completely focused old drivers with their hands at 10 and 2 (mainly because their heads are always at 6). Those same drivers performing complicated tasks while they drive is more horrifying than the exorcist. Why the urgency? Was he on his way to a hot date at the Bingo Hall? Or maybe the gefilte fish he had for lunch was too much even for him to bear alone in his car. I'm not sure where I stand on the elderly driving issue. It's complicated for sure. I can unequivocally say that I am 100% against old people driving and teeth brushing simultaneously. That may be my main campaign platform if I run for office.

Dwayne Perkins believes old farts should brush at home... Dwayne Perkins believes in our city... shouldn't you believe in him?

Dwayne Perkins: what this city's been missing.

Not-Chos

If the administration can admit that Iraq is not going as planned and the NBA can rethink this whole new basketball thing, then I think it's time for the rest of us to admit that nachos are not good. The whole nacho project has failed.

The concept of nachos is amazing, but in reality, every order of nachos turns into a frustrating high stakes game of edible Jenga, where the losers far outweigh the winners. Any given order has sixty chips and all the stuff either falls to the bottom or resides on eight chips. So that's fifty two chips that are either completely dry or have the faintest hint of cheese vapor. And if there's more than three people eating how do you divvy up the eight chips worth eating? Sometimes there's resentment and hurt feelings when one person takes a chip with two pounds of junk on it and boldly eats it while his friends have to gulp their drinks to help get down the dry salty chips that were left. Also, if you don't attack the nachos with a sense of purpose you end up with a bunch of cold cheese. Once the cheese cools, good luck picking up one chip without getting six of its buddies coming along for the ride.

There's hope though. I think we need to take all the nacho stuff (beans, chicken, cheese etc.) and mix it up with smaller pieces of broken up chips sprinkled in. Now you grab a fork and you're cooking with gas.

Spiraling Fame

A friend of mine has the most peculiar system of dealing with famous encounters. He's always impressed and somehow affected, even by B and C list stars. An A lister will make his day.

However, if he sees the same star again, A list or otherwise, he begins to feel that person really isn't all that. He basically downgrades them because if he has this kind of access to them then they must not be that famous or talented for that matter. And if he sees a celebrity for a third time in a short time span, then his feelings toward them almost turns into resentment. And a fourth would yield utter contempt. Even if he saw Oprah for a fifth time, I think he would want to fight her.

ME: Yo J., Cedric The Entertainer just walked in!!
J: You mean Cedric the getting on my

nerves. I saw that fool last week at the Barber Shop.

So, for my friend, seeing Rob Schneider for the first time would be equal to seeing Denzel for the second time. And seeing Screech for the first time would be like seeing Haile Berry for the 3rd time. And seeing anyone for the 5th time would be like stepping in hot gum.

Complicated stuff.

After Aftertaste

I was at a reception that had crab and garlic spread at the snack table. Needless to say, I dove right in. It's not everyday that I get to eat chives. The dip was great at first, but had a weird aftertaste. The only way to rid my mouth of the lingering pasty flavor was to eat more dip. You see my conundrum? I spent most of the night hovering by the dip table taking my mouth through the vicious taste cycle (yummy… crummy… yummy… crummy…) Basically, when something good has an aftertaste, you're forced to eat said thing til infinity. Or until you're asked to leave by the night security guard.

O. G. Willickers

I saw a man of about seventy walking on Ventura Blvd in Encino, CA. He was wearing an oversized black T-shirt, baggy black track pants, a du-rag and a gold chain. He had a white goatee with the mustache connected to the hair on his chin. Oh yeah, he was white.

I think I may have discovered the world's first wigger. Which begs the question:

Can a wigger predate hip hop? Maybe this guy ran in the bebop circles in the sixties and just flipped his style when rap came out. Or maybe he was just an average guy working his way through middle management, heard Rapper's Delight, and that was it. Up and traded in his khakis, Timex and classic rock for some baggy two-tone Lees, a blinged out Rollie, and dope beats. The hypest mid-life crisis ever. His wife probably took it the hardest.

Wife: Morty, just buy a red sports car like everybody else. People are talking.

Morty: They hate me cause they ain't me. I'm funky fresh yo!

Wife: Just Don't forget to fix the garage door, Morty 3000!

Young Frankenstein

My friend and I got out of my car in Los Angeles. Suddenly we heard the pitter-patter of a stampede approaching. Both being East Coasters, we braced ourselves for what seemed a full fledged bum-rush. We looked up with our fists at the ready only to see a lumbering, stout, big for his age junior high school kid running toward his parents' SUV behind us. This solitary kid was so uncoordinated that it sounded like a mob of angry river dancers were coming to avenge the death of a Leprechaun. Not to be mean, but you could take Frankenstein, get him piss drunk, then spin him around ten times really fast and make him run backwards down a steep hill and he would look like Fred Astaire compared to this kid.

When did kids forget how to run? Isn't that what kids do? They run. They run as a celebration of knowing nothing, having no cares, no bills and boundless energy. How does a kid get to junior high having not learned how to run?! I'm not asking for Carl Lewis. Just the base level of grace that even the stiffest of us was born with.

Sorry Los Angeles, but this kid wouldn't last a week in Brooklyn. Not unless he had enough lunch money for the entire school... everyday... including the teachers and lunch ladies.

This Round's On Me... Almost

At a bar with some people I just met. One guy stood up and offered to buy the next round of drinks. He pointed around the table taking orders. Sam Adams, Bud, Rum and Coke... he gets to me and I say "Diet Coke." He laughed and refused to by me a soda. He's all, "I'm not buying you a soda... I'll get you a drink though." Okay, maybe I was being a little girlie with the Diet Coke so I asked for a regular coke instead. That was my attempt to cowboy–up. He groaned, went to the bar and came back with a drink for everyone but me. HE WAS SERIOUS!! Basically this guy was saying, "I'll get you an expensive drink, but screw you if you think I'm going to buy you the cheapest thing this place sells." That's like saying, "Baby, I'll pay your rent, but you can go to hell if you think I'm buying you a shower curtain." Okay, maybe it's not like that, but you get my point.

Play Time is Over…Please

I saw some kids in the mall yesterday terrorizing their older cousin/aunt. The kids kept saying that they were bored and wanted to play. Let's put aside the fact that they were in a public place. Why do kids these days need constant amusement? Whatever happened to "Go sit down somewhere!" or the old staple "Take your ass outside!?" When did parents become content providers? The whole thing about being a kid is having an imagination. You're bored?! You're seven! Take this magical stick to the playroom and come back in four hours. PBS is boring to today's children because the camera is usually still. Today, kids need constant bombardment of changing camera angles and loud sounds. Pretty soon parents will have to produce short films to get their children to listen to them at all.

FATHER: Son, it's important that you

don't hit your sister... Here's a short film your mom and I shot to tell you why...now we haven't finished the credits and we're still waiting for legal to clear some of the songs, but hopefully it's good enough for you to stop kicking your sister in the head. Plus there's a preview of a film we shot about not talking back.

Enough With The Sauce

I went to a nice little Greek restaurant in Astoria, Queens. I ordered the lamb in Egglemons sauce. I think. My question is, how much sauce can be present before you legally have to call it soup? I think floating cabbage might be a dead giveaway that your "sauce" has outgrown that distinction. What if I had actually ordered soup? I probably would have had to pull my chair up to a tub. Eesh!

Gourmet Overpay

Have you seen the personal fitness area of your local gym/fitness facility lately? Does it not strike anyone as odd that the personal fitness area is the most barren part of the gym? The other parts have machines and do-dads of all kinds. But over in the VIP section of the gym you'll be lucky to find: some light hand weights, a few loose resistance bands and a bouncy bouncy ball pretending to be a workout ball of some sort. The people over in the VIP are always standing on one foot or squatting or jumping over things. Interesting looking stuff but hardly any of it involves the usage of the thousands of dollars worth of equipment chilling in the regular people section.

What message is the gym sending us?

You can pay a flat rate and use all the wonderful machines, but for a little more you can use this small section with stuff you probably already have at home?

Or maybe the message is...

Using those machines will get you in okay shape, but to really push your body into the stratosphere you'll need none of that.

I know those people can still use the cardio machines but it's clear that working out requires very little in the way of apparatuses....And they have the gall to show you this while charging you more for it.

This would be like a drug dealer charging one price for drugs but just a tad more for a hug or a stern talking to.

USER: Give me your strongest stuff.
DRUG DEALER: Well, I got some unconditional love but it's gonna cost you big time.

Diaper Dandy

Guys say they never look at other guys in the locker room and for the most part we don't. But for the observant amongst us it's hard to not see things out the corner of our forever roving eyes. Today, I caught a glimpse of an older gentleman at the gym taking off a diaper. I immediately turned away and pretended I didn't see it. If I'm lucky enough to get to the age where I need a diaper I would certainly want people to look away.

I was proud of this old man I don't even know. For most of you reading this, wearing a diaper would definitely be cause to shut down all public undressing. Put a fork in you, you're done. But this guy isn't going to let declining health send him off to pasture. It's like he's saying…"Fine, I wear diapers now but I got a life to live over here…"

Imagine finishing school, braving a couple of marriages, raising kids, paying a mortgage, sending the kids to school, paying for two daughters' weddings and at the end of all that you're handed a diaper.

A life of work and all you have to show for it are few ties, a box of Old Spice or Brut, a number one dad plaque and Huggies.

I say go out with a blaze.

Can't Win For Losing

We've all had one of those days.
Sunday, I caught a flat on the way to the
airport. I change the tire then get on
the expressway to be greeted with
not one but two major accidents. The
second takes up all but one lane. It's
Sunday at 8 in the morning and I'm in
bumper to bumper traffic. Too bad I
don't have a frisbee. I think I could get
a good throwing session going. The car
in front of me even has a dog. Note to
self: keep frisbee in car. I get to the
terminal fifteen minutes before my
flight leaves. They put me on standby
for the next flight. I'm still hopeful
because there's no line at security and
maybe I can run to the gate and plead
my case. I go through security and get
hit with the random search. Patted
down twice and all my bags opened and
rifled through. After I re-pack and
close all my bags, my plane has just
taken off. I exhale.

THE BIG APPLE

In a New York Minute

I'm standing at East 60th St. and 2nd Ave in New York City. Cars are racing off the Queensboro bridge at highway speeds, as if acclimating to local street traffic is not an option. This of course doesn't dissuade New Yorkers from anxiously standing on the curb waiting for the slightest break in traffic flow to rush across the street... against the light. So we're all standing there like the start of a 100 yard dash waiting for just the right moment. I look over and see a guy in a wheelchair focused and on the ready. A car passes with another car not two seconds behind it. Even for the bravest among us, this is not enough space to go. The guy in the wheelchair peels out like a bat out of hell and leaves us standing there eating metaphorical dust. He actually did a slight pop-a-wheelie. I swear the guy's wheelchair had a Hemi and a Nitrous Oxide system. You gotta love New York.

Do You Speak-a My Language

I was in a Laundromat in NYC a few months back. A cool place with front loaders. You gotta love the front loaders. They use less water and require less detergent. Don't try and figure that one out. You'll just give yourself a headache. In fact, I have a bottle of aspirin in my medicine cabinet labeled "Front Loader Paradox." The place is run by an older Asian woman. I think my clothes were still in pre-soak when an older white woman came in. Somehow her attempt to start pre-soak did not go as smoothly as mine. She had a laundry list of issues: trouble closing the door on one of her machines, needed change, had questions and concerns about when to put in fabric softener, etc. It seemed like maybe she was rich the day before but the bottom had just fell out and now she had to try her hand at semi-manual labor. Our laundry newbie asked the owner for help. The owner tried to help her, but there was definitely a disconnect. I guess the owner's strong accent combined with the lady's lack of general laundry knowledge made for frustration all around. The lady turned to me and said, "I really think if you're going to run a business here (America) you should speak English." I simply nodded in that 'I don't agree or disagree' kind of way.

Here's the kicker: as far as I could tell, the laundry owner was speaking English. The distressed washer asked for my help. I didn't think I was any more equipped than she was, but I gave it a shot. After all, I am quite skilled at charades and gestures and I always seem to know what Scooby Doo is saying. My requests to the laundry owner for change and credit for a broke machine seemed to get through. We began to make progress as a unit. A triumvirate of understanding, if you will. It was like when two of your friends aren't speaking to each other so they speak to each other through you.

The older white woman looked to me and said, "Do you speak Chinese?" I was baffled. Do I speak Chinese?! No, but good thing the laundry manager was speaking ENGLISH. I don't understand Chinese. I spoke English to the laundry manager and she spoke English back to me. I was translating English to English! The Laundrywoman only really needs to know maybe twenty different English phrases to do a bang up job managing the mat. To be fair, though, maybe I channeled the spirit of a Chinese person. Maybe I was speaking English in my head but Chinese came out of my mouth. Or maybe I just spoke a little slower, listened a little more intently, and took educated, laundry–related guesses.

Cough Up a Lung Where I'm From…

I'm in a bathroom in New York's Kennedy airport. A guy goes into the stall next to mine and starts coughing and hacking like there's no tomorrow. For some reason, people always do things extreme if they think tomorrow is in question. I've been considering blogging like there's no tomorrow but alas I'm too optimistic and I believe there will be a tomorrow. So instead I blog like there's probably a next week. But I digress. The sound of this guy's cough was more terrifying than Stevie Wonder driving your daughter's school bus. It's like his esophagus was lined with barbed wire and rusty screws. He coughed in hi-fi dolby surround sound. I'm sure his colon was holding on for dear life. In the midst of the hack symphony another guy two stalls over says, "That's it buddy, get it out!"

I left the bathroom, mainly because I was finished but also because the sound of the hacking was about to make me dry heave. I didn't stick around to confirm but I'm pretty sure the guy who delivered the pep talk did not even know the guy coughing up his innards. Us New Yorkers, we give and keep giving. Only in New York would a guy be possibly dying and people give him encouraging words and think that's enough.

New Yorker: That knife wound is pretty deep. Good luck with that pal... Taxi!

Radio Raheem

I was in NYC two weeks ago. I'm on the
corner of 34th st and 7th Ave. Very
busy... the city that never sleeps... blah,
blah, blah. I'm talking on my phone
when a Black guy walks by wearing
Gazelle glasses (same glasses worn by
DMC of the RUN–DMC rap legends).
He's donning a Boston Bruin gold and
black jumpsuit with gold shoelaces in
his black Nikes. And caring a boombox.
In the days of Ipods and complete music
catalogues on keychains, this guy is
sticking to his boombox ghetto blaster
that plays cassettes. So instantly I like
this guy. As an aside I can guarantee
you that this guy doesn't like the Boston
Bruins and has never even seen a
hockey game. I just know this kind of
homey. He's probably seen every Kung
fu movie ever made and is a card
carrying member of the Wu–Tang Clan
fan club.

So the guys draws closer and I hear that

he's blasting Public Enemy's "Fight The Power." I give him the ghetto "what's up" nod. He stops and puts his radio near my phone so my friend on the other end can hear. At this close range I see that he's written "Radio Raheem" on the speakers of the boom box. We give each other a pound (modified handshake where we both made fists and touched them together in the most masculine way this can be done). Then he walked away in his quest to bless the rest of the city with his message, one block at a time. Now that's the real surreal life. I nominate Radio Raheem to be an official super hero... taking out all Sucker MC's and wackness wherever they may hide, for the betterment of all mankind.

Metro Pimp

I was riding on a bus in New York City. A guy sat next to me wearing a huge full length fur coat with a matching fur hat. Underneath that he had on a red three piece suit with orange stripes. He donned gold chains, bracelets, and wore alligator shoes. He had to pick up the back of his coat– like a bride has to pick up her train to get in the limo– just to sit down! On the bus, people!! Pimpin' ain't easy.

PIMP: Where's my money?!

HO: I'm a little short, baby, but–

PIMP: Short my ass! Is Metro Pimp gonna have to choke a bitch?!

HO: Just give me some time, daddy.

PIMP: Time is what I don't have. My transfer expires in five minutes. Look, I gotta take the M3 bus uptown, ya dig, then two trains to see my other ho. I'm catching the 6:45 downtown bus, I'll be back here at 9:00. Bitch betta have my money then! But uh, if you don't see me that means I missed the 6:45 and should be touching down around 9:30. If that's the case, then, well… have my money then, bitch! See, messing with you done made me lose my transfer. You got change for a dollar?

New York Games

I was on the Roosevelt Island Tram in New York City. You may remember this as the red cable car at the end of Spiderman where Spidey and the Green Goblin got it poppin.' The tram was docked and the operator closed the doors so the exodus could begin. Just then, a fifty–something woman, half a block away, wearing a business jacket, skirt and high heels looked up and started to run toward the tram like she was on fire and had never seen the stop, drop and roll PSA. She was trying to catch the tram before it left but her chances were slim. This did not deter her and her efforts were rewarded as the tram did not take off right away and the operator opened the doors to let her in. She was panting, flushed, and sweaty, but victory was hers. I love New Yorkers. Only in New York would a woman dressed to the nines put all pride and personal safety aside just to catch mass transit. She could have just as easily been panting, flushed, and sweaty standing all by her lonesome waiting for the next Tram. Nothing ventured, nothing gained.

This got me thinking. I know the X-Games are taking off, but I propose we have the New York Games. The games would all be New York based challenges.

Here's a list of the inaugural competitions:
• The stop a subway door from closing

event
• The hail a taxi with 8 bags in your hand event
• The crossing against the light event (participants would have to sign a waiver)
• The ignore the homeless singing quartet in the subway event
• The haggle down a street vendor on a fake Rolex event
• The standing up on a moving bus, with no shocks, without holding on event

Get it Poppin': To start something on a high level. In this case Spiderman and Green Goblin started fighting, an epic battle indeed.

PSA: Public Service Announcement: Little golden nuggets of advice the government gives to the people so the public can stay informed and safe. In this case, if you're on fire it's better to roll on the ground than to run. (See Richard Pryor)

Not So Rude Awakening

I was outside in Brooklyn a few days ago. I was holding my little 2 & 1/2 year old cousin while he slept. As I held him, people from surrounding porches spoke loudly and played card games. Kids ran noisily through the running fire hydrant. Several cars crept by blasting hip–hop, reggae, or reggaeton, stopping before the fire hydrant, speakers blaring, to close their windows to avoid getting their plush interiors wet. Through all of this, my cousin slept like a bear in hibernation. Then… from two blocks away, the faint whisper of the ice cream truck song became barely audible. My little cousin jumped up in my arms fully awake and ready for ice cream. It was almost like he snapped out of being hypnotized but instead of "on the count of three you will wake up and not remember this…" the trigger was on the sound of "do do da do da do da do da do do do do…"

When he starts school, my suggestion would be an ice cream truck alarm clock.

Foaming At The Mouth

So my tour of the quaintest coffee shops in America continues. I recently found a little jewel of a place in New York City called Starbucks. I think it may really catch on. Even the other one directly across the street seemed delightful.

The woman in front of me ordered one of those hot beverages that gets topped of with the foam art work. I think some sort of leaf is the artistic aim of most baristas. But the girl behind the counter announced to me and the drink orderer, but more to me, that she could make the foam form the shape of a penis. Now that's what I call talent. I was at a lost for words. Every now and then someone says something to you that simply has no comeback. Like the talking computer in the movie "War Games" my brain raced through all the possible responses and the counter responses each response might provoke. In the end the only suitable thing to do was to smile and say....

ME: *Wow! (pause) Yeah...um...can I get a Grande Chai...*

I know some of my readers may think she was flirting with me. Perhaps, but where do you go from there? A whisper can eventually become a scream. A scream can only become something dogs and dolphins respond to.

Anything I said also was in jeopardy of making me sound creepy. Salesman have bait and switch. Women have flirt with and creepify. I pictured me saying something just to keep that genitalia foam art ball in the air and her doing an emotional 180 and looking at me like I was a perv with a long buttoned up trench coat on in July.

Many a men have taken the playful sexy discourse bait only to find themselves looked down upon and ostracized from the general community. I didn't have game but I had my dignity and standing in the community.

One faithful reader, Doug Stolland, thinks I should have said, "Really? Because I have a penis that can create foam art."

Touche, too bad you weren't there Doug. Although, I think that may have freaked her out and left me all alone on creep island.

Almost Famous

Sometimes I forget that people may know me from TV. I get recognized once every 22 business days for comedy/TV. So, when someone is looking at me I can't assume they know me from comedy. I always think I went to school with them or maybe we took an interpretive dance class together back in '96. I'm just afraid that one day I'll be wearing white sunglasses with a diamond studded belt buckle and someone will say,

FAN: Dwayne right?

...and then I go to sign their forehead and they say...

FAN: Get away from me you freak! You dated my sister, dummy. I just didn't recognize you with the Judy Garland shades on. Wait 'til I tell her how lame and Hollywood you are now...

So, I always exhaust all possible ways a person could know me before I settle in on comedy/TV. Sometimes it gets pretty ridiculous but I'd rather do that then get all Lamesville.

FAN2: No...it wasn't Tae Kwon Do class...This is killing me ...How do I know you?
ME: You ever ride the B36 bus in Brooklyn back in the late eighties?

But even worse than possibly being a jerk to someone I should know is when a person in, say the subway in New York stares at me. In my head I get all "Brooklyn."

ME: (in my head)What is this fool looking at?! You wanna go homey?!

I actually plan the whole fight out in my head. Maybe I'll foot swipe him...no...I'll jab him in the throat first then kick him in the shin...or maybe I should just punch him as hard as I can in the ear...

On several occasions I've been going through my fight plan only to have the guy walk over and say…

FAN3: Yo sun, you mad funny B! I like the thing you do…

Of course then I feel like crap. This guy loves my comedy maybe even reads my blogs… and I was going to punch him in the throat. You can take the boy out of Brooklyn…

A Night in The Projects

So I spent the night at my cousin's place in New York. The plan was to get up early and leave out with him. When he went to work, I'd go to "work".   I put mine in quotes because it involves drinking copious amounts of tea and I can leave whenever I want and I don't really report to anyone. Actually, that makes it harder for me in the big picture. I know no one clocking in with old man Wilson busting his hump wants to hear about the big picture.

I got up early even though getting to sleep was tough. Not to sound uppity but my cousin has roaches. He lives in the Projects. Everyone in the projects has roaches. It's not a cleanliness thing. There is literally no margin for error. A wet sponge can be a supermarket for roaches. Okay maybe a bodega but you get the point. One has to be cleaner in the PJs than anywhere else. And even if your place is immaculate you're basically temporarily discouraging the roaches. They may skip over your place but they're still always in striking distance should you throw an orange peel in the garbage or drop a few crumbs while chomping on a cinnabon. Like sitting in a train car with houligans harrassing people, you do your best and hope they leave you be.

I'm not sure why it affected me so. I lived in the projects and did battle with the creepy crawlers for the first 18 years of my life. Was I afraid of roaches or what my brain associates them with? Struggle, violence, failed electronics. (roaches were the first Gremlins except you couldn't feed them anytime) Or maybe I was worried with what I've become. Someone phased by roaches. Someone who's lost his edge. Although ultimately our goal is to lose our edge. Sucess has a reverse correlation with edge. It actually took me five minutes to kill a roach. I forgot how resourceful and tricky they can be.

To effectively kill roaches your ruthlessness has to be on swol. I should also mention that ever since Men in Black came out I've been a little afraid that killing a roach could have bigger implications.

This all made a girl named Carmen Soto rush to mind. She basically saved my life or at least my entire 6th grade year. See, Carmen sat next to me and once saw a roach come out of my bookbag. We locked eyes and she said and did nothing. I was filled with terror and squashed the roach with my hand (I had edge back then.) Carmen did not blow up my spot and I am forever grateful. Knowing what I know now about women and people in general, I should've proposed to her right then. That kind of restraint and compassion doesn't grow on trees. She was probably fighting the same fight I was. She lived in the project across the street from mine. I'm sure she made some guy very happy. Carmen's kindess put a smile on my face and my preoccupation with things that go crunch in the night subsided and I fell asleep. I'll check my bag thoroughly before I go back to LA.

TRAVELS

Don't Make Me Repeat Myself

I was recently (drum roll please....) on a plane and the flight attendants were about to begin the 2nd snack service. One flight attendant stood at the front of the cabin and made everyone look up. She then, loudly, deliberately and very condescendingly began to tell us our snack options. She took a tone I imagine you would have had to take to get a point across to a young Tom Arnold...or current day Tom Arnold now. She clearly was saying without saying that she would tell us these options once and only once. God forbid she has to repeat the options to some slacker not paying attention. She went down the list like each item was a step in diffusing a bomb and to miss one would mean ka-boom.

FLIGHT ATTENDANT: You can get Sun Chips (hold it up, look around, pause... hold...and release). Chewy Granola bar (hold it up, look around, pause...hold... and release)....

Of course I did not want her patronizing to go in vain. There was a reason she talked down to us. A reason she treated us like one would an autistic classroom, sans the affection and love. And that reason is Dwayne Perkins. The other passengers, scared to death of the Snack Nazi, ordered swiftly. When she finally got to my row I looked up, rubbing my chin in deep indecisiveness, and asked "What are the choices again?" (smile,pause...hold...)

There was a look of horrific disbelief on her face. Clearly, she thought the five minute Power Point snack presentation would spare her from dweebs like me making her go through the drill again. She took a deep breath and ran down the list again

FLIGHT ATTENDANT: Sir! You can have Sun Chips (hold it up...evil look at me...

pause…hold…release…)

ME: Tough choice…What do you recommend?

She pressed her lips together so tightly, I thought her top and bottom lip were going to switch places.

Muah.

Freaks and Geeks

The Daniel Tosh tour bus pulled into San Diego Saturday morning just as the changing of the guards was taking place.

If the freaks come out at night, and I believe they do, then dawn is that odd time when the goodie goods and the freaks intersect. It's a wonderful time of day. Like a shift change in the factory of life. The not ready for prime timers give way to the "Up And At 'Em" crowd. At dawn, the best of the best cross paths with the freakiest of the freaky or, if it's the weekend, the hardiest of the partiers.

The morning joggers, draped in gore-tex and the latest offering in running technology on their feet, weave thru cleaning crews, empty bottles and the half awake folks dressed in their party outfits from the night before.

I don't mean to have a pro morning person slant. I doubt the people heading to bed would trade the previous night's debauchery for a running high. And the early birds don't mind dozing off after the evening news to get up at 6am and face the world.

We need both factions. They both serve a purpose to the economy and culture on the whole. My goal has always been to run wild with the freaks but get up in time to do a mild jog with the chipper AM crew. It's the great party hard–get up early conundrum that no one has quite figured out. Enter coffee, concealer and a well placed power nap.

I love the night life but I also love to boogie to a coffee shop at the crack of ass on my quest to be the story teller with the most–est. I've had a good run and I will miss the short skirts and don't get me started on the cut off jeans shorts so short that the pockets are longer than the jeans. I'll miss seeing girls hobbling on one heel with their slightly less drunk girlfriends holding them up. But my place is with the morning crew the people who see army commercials and say "Is that all they do before 6 am?!" I'll have to find a way to wear out my inner night owl during the day so he doesn't keep me up til 3am watching youtube rap battles. (Shout out to Murder Mook)

A shift change is a comin'. Good morning.

Signed, Sealed…No Delivery

So I had a show in Lake Havasu, home of the "Girls Gone Wild" series, last night. This is my fourth show in Havasu and I've yet to see a "Girls Gone Wild" taping. I have however seen a lot of wild girls. Havasu minus spring breakers is like hanging with Randy Macho Man Savage when he's not in costume and hasn't just snapped into a Slim Jim. A bit of a let down. Don't get me wrong, I like the place. It's beautiful and tranquil but I think the locals maybe try too hard to keep the party going long after the spring breakers have left. It's sad really. Like that guy who won't leave a house party. The hosts are cleaning up and he's still doing the Cha Cha Dance, by himself, sans Cha Cha song, while instead the Sham Wow infomercial blares in the background.

HOST: How does he know when to turn

it out, or hop 3 times?

It's hard for a small local population to sustain the party rep of thousands of young college kids. But damn if they don't try. Against all logic and promises I had made to myself, I went with the other comic to a local bar called BJs. It's almost a ritual of ours at this point. One of those things you do for absolutely no reason other than that you did it in the past. It was what it always has been…sloppiness epitomized and scores of people who should have been cut off before they left the house. One guy recognized me from TV. Game begin. He was a big fan and was genuinely happy to meet me as I was genuinely happy to meet him. He fawned over me a bit which made other people notice. Next thing I know, I'm signing autographs for people who don't even know me.

GUY WHO DOESN'T KNOW ME: Please make that out to Gary…Who are you again?

But here's the kicker...my one true fan was there with his girlfriend. Not sure if she was a fan. What I am sure of is that she asked me to sign her birth control case. Picture a small wallet with no credit cards but get out of jail free pills inside. I guess she won't lose it? I'm not sure what the subtext was but I was uncomfortable as hell. My fan was cool with it though. It's one of those things that seem disrespectful but because it was so random there was no precedent to judge it against.

ME: Yo dawg! I think you need to check you girl...I guess...maybe...who do I make this out to?

This sparks the debate that will grip our nation for some time to come. What's more disrespectful to a boyfriend: His girl having her boob signed or her birth control case?

Shout out to: Styles Night Club, BJ's,

Dallas, Chris from the BX, and Andrew (names changed to protect the guilty 😃

White Castle Dreaming

Anyone who once lived in an area where there were White Castles and now lives out of Castle range should be able to relate to this one.

When you live near a White Castle you hardly ever eat there. If you do it's probably after 2am, everything else is closed, and you're in an altered state. I bet White Castle makes 80% of their money between 1am and 5am. If you walk into a White Castle before 11pm they ask you to fill out a survey. They want to know who you are and what you're about.

RICKY RICARDO: 6pm and you went to White Castle?! Lucy, you got some splaining to do!

I drove past a White Castle in Columbus Ohio and nearly lost my mind. That grease nostalgia is a mother. You have to order like it's your last meal too. The burgers are only 75 cents...this could be the last time you ever eat at the Castle... so of course, gluttony ensues.

So I order chicken rings, because I can, 4 burgers and 4 cheeseburgers and head back to my hotel room for the throw down. Tragically, I got back to my room to find I had no ketchup. I tried to plow ahead. But after 4 burgers I felt I was cheating myself. I couldn't go on living a lie. Who was I kidding? I needed ketchup and I needed it bad. So I go back 2 exits on the highway to the white castle. Sure, I could have just asked for ketchup to finish off the remaining 4 burgers in my room but I wasn't sure ketchup would make-up for the burgers being room temperature.

So, just to be safe, I ordered 3 more burgers and 3 more cheeseburgers and loaded up on 12 burgers worth of ketchup. The trip back was well worth it and I achieved total grease nirvana. Even the room temperature ones were dy-no-mite.

Gracias Castillo Blanco!

If you have some time to spare, and as a reader of my blog you must, check out the White Castle Timeline of all the Castle's milestones.

http://whitecastle.com/_pages/ timeline.asp

Big Shout to Heidelberg College in Tiffin, OH.

Freestyle Slave

I was in a bar in Indiana hanging with the staff from Morty's Comedy Joint. Deon, a young comic from Indy started a freestyle cipher* with me and another bar patron we didn't know. I'm from Brooklyn so I'm always up for a little "yes yes yall"**

It went as well as could be expected from 2 drunk guys and sub-par lyricist (me) with alternative music blaring in the background from the jukebox. These things usually peter out fairly quickly. It's like 3 minutes of glory followed by a realization that, oh yeah this is kinda hard....that's why Jay-Z gets the big bucks. (well that and his clothing line, nightclub, sneaker deal, and his own vodka)
So, at the logical conclusion of our impromptu cipher, Deon gracefully made his way back over to the dart board. Leaving me with Freestylin'

Stranger Number 1. (FSN1)

QSN: Bars are like social circuit training. There's the bar, the dart board, the photo hunt/trivia game, the juke box, the pool table, the popcorn machine and so on. You get your fill at a station then you move on. Sometimes though, a person overstays their welcome at one station. Like a guy who won't leave the Bar. He's getting drunk too quick cause he won't rotate. Plus he's hogging the filthy peanut bowl. Hey buddy leave some germs for the rest of us. It's the equivalent of the guy in the gym that will only work out his back. His back is tremendous but he can't open a jar of mayonnaise. You like dry sandwiches my ass. Here's a mayonnaise packet Mr. Backy.

So I'm there with FSN1. I figured I would oblige him for another minute and switch stations. Freestyling at a bar is like that guy in the gym doing karate kicks by the chin up bar. It's an unsanctioned station he just made up on the fly. You can put up with it for a while but eventually he has to stop the capoeira*** or apply for an official station.

As I tried to gracefully end our cipher it became apparent that FSN1 didn't want it to end. This guy had no freestyle etiquette.

ME: Hey man good stuff but I think I'm gonna–
FSN1: Good stuff call your bluff. I'm more than enough. Believe I'm rough.–
ME: Okay that was hot but, it's a little late now–
FSN1: Late now. I'm great now. Pulled back my jammie and let it go blaouw!–
FSN1: Now you're walking away. I got more to say. And when the cipher is hot, I flow for days.

I had to keep freestylin' with this guy for another 15 minutes. A very costly freestyle indeed...

* A cipher is when two or more people stand, usually in a circle or something close to it, and take turns saying rhymes. Checki it
http://www.youtube.com/watch?v=8gsKSFzMtiE

**yes, yes, yall – intro or placeholders rappers say to keep the energy up until they start saying their next offering. Or a button put at the end of a rap offering.

*** capoeira – An Afro-Brazilian dance form that incorporates self-defense maneuvers. And many say is what break dancing was born out of.
http://www.youtube.com/watch?v=DdZXp0Tq6Jk

Wake Me Up Before You Go Go

I have an uncanny ability to wake–up on an airplane just as the flight attendants pass my seat with drinks and snacks. It may be some deep rooted fear of missing out or maybe my subconscious' way of getting more bang for my buck. You know that guy in the movies you think is dead until you reach over him for the gold and in a last ditch effort his arm comes to life and pulls you down. Well, that's me in my aisle seat when my row is passed. Not so fast missy....

ME: Next time you pass a man over... make sure he's sleep first. I'll have a Ginger Ale...Yes the whole can.

I could stay up 48 hours straight, then get jumped into a gang and take 3 Ambiens immediately after that, get on a plane and I still wouldn't miss the 1st and 2nd snack service. If I'm ever in a coma, before you pull the plug, just try wheeling a snack cart by me first.

NURSE: Mr Perkins! You're awake?!?
ME: (cough, cough) What..what happened…where am (cough, cough) I… let me get a Ginger Ale…(cough cough) the whole can please.

In The Presence of Royalty

I can't believe I forgot to tell this story earlier. I was recently sitting in coach on a packed plane before takeoff. As I walked out of the bathroom after my customary pre–takeoff tinkle, who do I see walking down the aisle toward me?; none other than Hip Hop God, Doug E Fresh.Doug is Hip Hop royalty in every sense of the word. He's the original beat boxer and the best entertainer of all time in Hip Hop. He introduced the world to Slick Rick and his song "The Show" is still one of the top 5 hip hop songs of all time.

Yes, even better than "This Is Why I'm Hot" or "Booty Meat".

I couldn't believe I was going to walk past the great Doug E Fresh. Even more unbelievable was the fact that he was in coach. I know not all Hip Hop pioneers made the money they deserved and maybe Doug was just practicing a sensible MST (Money Saving Technique) but it just felt wrong for one of Rap's best ambassadors to be with the rest of the dregs in coach.

I casually mentioned to the flight attendant as Mr. Fresh walked toward us...

ME: Oh s&@t! That's Doug E Fresh, The world's greatest entertainer!

Flight Attendant: That guy?

ME: Yep, he's a friggin' legend, the best of all time. The best I tell ya!!

Then I casually walked by Doug E. I didn't want to bother him so I just gave him a pound and I said Shalom.

The plane was packed and the only way to accommodate some of the people waiting on standby was to bump some people up to First Class to make room in Economy. I looked up and saw that the flight attendant I just spoke to was escorting Doug E Fresh up to First Class. I would like to think my jock riding (enthusiasm for the ebonically challenged) helped get Doug up in First Class where he deserves to be on any plane...and in our hearts.

I felt good, like I had corrected a grave error and it didn't matter to me that the guy sitting next to me smelled like chicken noodle soup and not in a good way.

6 minutes Doug E Fresh, you're in First!

I Get A Kick Out of You

I was sitting in the window seat on a plane yesterday. A woman with two children sat behind me. I usually go to sleep before take off so my eyes were closed. I didn't use my innate Jedi skills to ascertain there was a woman with kids behind me. No, her youngest son's screaming combined with the older boy saying "Mom!" over and over told the story before I could use the force. We hadn't even taken off and the gauntlet had been thrown. The boy's screaming Vs. my much needed cat nap.

I gladly accepted the challenge. If you can sleep standing up on the E express while a homeless man plays the banjo you gotta like your chances against a screaming 3 year old. Sure enough I jumped out to an early lead as I drifted off, amidst the screaming, just as the plane pulled away from the terminal.

But young Sebastian had more tricks up his sleeve. As we reached cruising attitude, I was awakened by our antagonist kicking into my chair. Foul Ball! Even the New York City panhandlers don't kick. Around the same time the woman next to me took ill. Her husband stood up and relinquished the aisle seat to her.   The middle seat?   Well that went to the oxygen tank they bought out for the woman. Meanwhile Sebastian went all out and by now was jumping over the seats and looking down at me. He even touched my head a few times. Which is understandable. Perhaps he never touched a black man's hair before? I'm sure each of my White readers remembers the first time they touched black hair. Young Sebastian didn't feel like waiting until Junior High to see what the spongy afro is all about.

So now not only was sleeping difficult, it would also be somewhat insensitive. Add to that the fact that the gallon of Chamomile tea I drank before I boarded wanted out but I didn't want to climb over a sick woman connected to an oxygen tank and you see how Sebastian was going to win. I was surprisingly and remarkably calm for a guy who had to go to the bathroom and had a 3 year old terrorizing him.

I never did get back to sleep but Young Sebastian did...just as we landed. Oh hell naw!
After the flight his mom did apologize and seemed confused and impressed by my calm. She was looking at me like people look at Batman after he saves them. Who was the calm man?!...I did look at Sebastian a few times and he stopped dead in his tracks. Without a male voice, someone truly able to ignore him or someone willing to fully follow through on consequences his

mom has her hands full.

My friends are often shocked by how Zen I am about some things and at the same time so unyielding on other things.

Case in point: The time I threatened to burn down a sports bar over a discrepancy around the inclusion of a side salad with a sandwich (You had to be there).

Where Are They Now

It's always cool to see the people you saw on your outbound flight, on your returning flight. It's not cosmic but it sort of builds community. Albeit in your mind.

DWAYNE'S MIND: There's a person who agrees that a 4 day stint in Albuquerque is exactly enough time. I wonder what else we agree on? I wonder if George is his favorite Beatle...

I was lucky enough to have two parties fly on the same plane as me going and coming.

One of which has already made my blog. Remarkably my favorite young seat kicker from two blogs ago, Sebastian, was on my return flight. His mom gave me an exuberant hello. Oddly, I was just as happy to see her and Mr. Terror himself. It's like the 4 hours of seat kicking had bonded us like men who have been in war together. They can go years without talking but their bond will always be there. For Sebastian and Me, our epic battle 30 thousand feet above ground will forever link us. Or at least our link survived the weekend.

Given my history with Sebastian it would have been understandable if I let out a shriek and ran away in fear like Linda Hamilton in Terminator 2 at the sight of Arnold Schwarzenegger. But Linda didn't have to run. For Arnold was a good guy in Terminator 2. As was Sebastian in our sequel. I didn't sit near him but I did go to the bathroom twice and both times he was sleeping like… well…a baby. The people on the return plane didn't even know his name. On the outbound flight not only did everyone know his name, several people could do a dead on impression of his mom telling him to stop.

I'm glad fate let me meet Sebastian again and see another side of him. Maybe even his true side. His mom did say he was a good boy. Seeing is believing.

How about that? A sequel that was better than the original.

Take the Order and Run

At the Popeye's in the US Airways terminal at the Raleigh airport...

QSN: Why is every other airport shop employee Ethiopian? I'm talking every airport in the country. Seems like such an odd market to corner. How did this come to be? Are the Airport HR guys waiting for these Ethiopians on the runway with a paper hat, khakis, and a polo shirt when they arrive?

HR GUY: Welcome to America.... land of opportunity... no, you won't be needing a cab.

So the guy ahead of me at Popeye's was being helped by one of the aforementioned Ethiopians. She charged him for a chicken biscuit meal but all he wanted was the sandwich. She tried giving him the meal but he was intent on only being charged for the sandwich. Fear washed over her.

She bit her lower lip and batted her
eyes. I detected either flirting or
desperation on her part to convince this
guy to just man–up to the meal deal.
He wouldn't bite.

Dude! You want to do a void at the
airport Popeye's?!... on a credit card!!
Even without the language barrier
you're talking about a transaction that's
Triple Lindy difficult. I could see in her
eyes that she was in uncharted territory.
I had two hours before my flight left and
I was already past security but suddenly
making my flight was no longer a
certainty. The manager had to come
out with sleeves rolled. I was about to
just give the guy a buck fifty and take
the hash browns and coffee off his
hands. The Popeye's line grew and
grew as the manager and employee
undertook the void process. The line
almost went back through security. I
think the last few people in line had to
re-show their boarding pass and take

off their shoes.

BTW: The Popeye's chicken biscuit was delish. Bad eating never tasted so good. And I have no problem with the employees being Ethiopian... just wondering how that came to be.

I Reminisce, I Reminisce

I'm sitting in a hip coffee shop in the Haight Asbury section of San Francisco. I caught some flack for being in a city as "Peace and Love" as San Fran and going to Starbucks. Guilty as charged but convenience is America's number one vice and I am American after all. Throw in the fact that there were three Starbucks within a block of my hotel and maybe you guys can cut me some slack?

I tried to make amends. I'm in the area where the "Hippie" was born and I'm sitting in a coffee shop called "Coffee To The People". I'm typing with one hand and my other hand is raised above my head in a tight fist. Forgive me but I left my black beret in Los Angeles.
I'm sitting a few tables away from a guy who may have a few stories to tell from the old Hippie days. His teeth game is not up to snuff and his hair is mutinous

but he's definitely lucid and not homeless. They're playing folksy music that seems like the same music that blared from rooftops here in the 60's and 70's. I didn't recognize all the songs but they sounded like songs from bands that maybe played the daytime small stage at the original Wood Stock. That is, if they had a daytime small stage a the original Wood Stock.

I can tell homey is being taken back to his youth. His face is lighting up and becoming brighter with each new song. It's like he's saying…"That's my s%$t!"

QSN: When I have kids I don't plan on letting them curse in my presence except for when a great song comes on the radio. They will be allowed to say "That's my s%$t!" Because I believe in leading by example and I know that's one curse scenario I can't give up. It has to be a good song though. Try that with the Macarena and someone's getting licks.

Back to dude. He's thinking about the good ole days. Maybe a girl he dated when this song was out...that concert for the ages...manageable marijuana....

I feel bad because he just caught me looking and has become self conscious. He's still rocking out but no longer unabashedly. I didn't mean to cut short your flashback broham.

Rock Like I'm not watching.

Peace, Love and Home Keys

I was walking along Haight St. in San Francisco playing an involuntary game called "Dodge The Panhandlers Who Look Broke By Choice." I'm actually pretty good at it. I don't have an extra cig, as I don't smoke and they always ask for "spare" change. But I had an airplane Sky Mall Magazine in my book bag. The Sky Mall sells Wind Powered Cell phone chargers, Inflatable Movie Screens and so much more. Can I really have spare change with these products available but not yet in my possession? I dare say until I have a Titanium Head Massager then no, I don't have spare change.

On the corner of Haight and Asbury I spied a Theolonius Monk looking brother sitting at a small desk typing on a typewriter. It's hard to be weird on Haight street but Mr. Happy Fingers was succeeding with flying colors. This guy had somehow scored a 3rd grade school desk and a 1960's typewriter. That alone is no small feat but to then set up shop outside on a busy corner well that gets your face on Weird Mount Rushmore.

It took all I had to not ask him what he was working on. Admittedly, I was hating. I knew he wanted people to ask him and that's the very reason I didn't. You want to act like sitting outside and typing is normal? Then I will too. I had the mind to go get my own typewriter and join him. Not so special now huh?

ME: Just typing on the corner too…Ya know, just like we used to do in the old country…can you spare some whiteout? …I do need it!

The only problem with that is what if my action was mistaken for paying homage instead of it's intended goal of mockery. What if more people joined in on the ridiculous PDT (Public Display of Typing?) This guy would become our

Forest Gump. I was tyyyyyping!!!

In the end I guess this guy won. I did write a blog about him after all. Whatever he was working on is probably not going to be any good. Besides the obvious reasons he also didn't have an outline.

WORLD TRAVELS

It's Gonna Be a Bumpy Ride

I got off an airplane in Ocho Rios, Jamaica. The cruise ship I was boarding in Jamaica had arranged a ride for me. I get to ground transportation and a cabbie gives me a nod and points at me. I'm thinking this must be my ride, he probably notices me from my picture. We get to his car and something tells me to confirm…

Me: Are you the person who's supposed to pick me up?
Him: The what?

Thank heavens I figured that one out. I didnt want to pay for a two hour cab drive to Montego Bay when someone had already paid for me. After I told my almost–cabbie that I was all set and had a prearranged ride, he asked me if I needed some Ganja. I got the feeling this guy could get me whatever I wanted.

"Lost episodes of Mash with directors comments? Just give me 10 minutes, mon...respect!"

After fifteen minutes, I finally find the guy that is actually there to pick me up. He tells me to hold tight. I held tight for an hour and a half.

Normally a wait that long would have drove me crazy. But "Welcome to Jam-Rock"* played three times. And there's no way you can be upset when that song is on. "What? Im fired?" ...'Out in The Street...They call it Murderrrrrrr...' "That's my song!! Let's talk severance pay after the last few Jamaica, Jamaicas..."

Plus, the people-watching was primo.

So about twenty-five failed Ganja offers later, my top-flight cabbie finally came back and we were off to Montego Bay. Most of the two hour trip was on a pitch black road with one lane going in each direction. I think they drive on the other side of the road in Jamaica, but as my driver spent equal time on both sides, I can't really say. What I know is I spent most of the trip wondering why there were headlights approaching us. You want to let people do their jobs but at the same time you feel inclined to mention that another vehicle is coming and two cars cant occupy the same space at the same time.

Me: Umm, I think we might need to get over... those are headlights not taillights we're coming up on...

Cabbie: Quite so. Easy Star! Me been driving this road for a long time, Mon. I can make this trip with me eyes closed.

I think he was talking from experience. It got to a point where near –misses were a relief. A few times, I really thought I was dead. I was actually looking around for my body because I thought surely I'm only spirit at this point. Twenty minutes in I knew if a crash didn't kill me then cardiac arrest would. So I closed my eyes and just listened to sports radio about how the West Indies Cricket Team is underachieving and needs to give it to the Netherlands. I thought, not what I want my last listening to be, but at least it wasnt techno. Needless to say we got to Montego Bay and all's well that ends well. I do think Six Flags could open up a new ride called From Ocho Rios to Montego Bay. I would put it up against any rollercoaster.

* Welcome to Jam Rock by Damian Marley. Hot track for sure.

Balance Is Key

I stood on the District line train in London's Underground ready to disembark, not holding on to anything, applying lotion and lip balm as the train pulled into Victoria. I finished up my beauty regimen as the train jerked to a stop and was taken back to my childhood in New York City...

When I was 8 I thought the worst thing in the world was holding on while the trained moved. It wasn't about me being a big boy it was more about proving to me and my mom that I was a super hero in training with death defying balance. My mom would beg me to hold on and I would ignore her. Sometimes being a super hero means blocking out the naysayers, even if they gave you life. My mom is truly one of the most patient people I have ever known so she wasn't the type to put down the iron hammer. She let my training run its course. That is until I slammed into the shin of an unsuspecting passenger. Then she would rough me up a bit, more out of social obligation than anything else, and make me take a seat.

Even a super hero knows when to retreat so I would humbly take my seat and vow to continue my training at a later date. That later date was usually 10 minutes later.

As I successfully applied Vaseline intensive care to my hands and Burt's Bees to my lips without crashing into another passenger I smiled and in my head said, "look Ma, no hands."

My persistence mixed with my mother's patience has made me a top notch train surfer. It's like I trained in Maui on a rickety surf board and now I'm surfing in the mild Atlantic with top notch equipment. The London Tube didn't stand a chance. Thanks Mom.

Video Killed the Parenting Star

I think technology has made parenting a lot harder. Says the non-parent. You don't have to go to PTA meetings to know the internet is a doozie. However, There's a another piece of technology that's a bit more stealth in how it undermines parenting.

I was riding on the London Undergound. I shared a car with a couple with two kids, one in a stroller and a very active toddler. Now, I've shared with you my train antics as a lad. How I refused to hold on to the pole to demonstrate my supreme super hero balance.

My mom suffered my poppycock with amazing grace and patience. Though, I do think my mom would have drawn the line at me going vertical. The young boy hoisted himself all the way up a pole. I was equally amazed by his upper body strength as I was his mom and dad's compliance. The boy then, after several failed attempts, swung himself from the vertical pole to the horizontal one above his parents' heads. I'm not sure I could do that now! So the lad is definitely showing talent for gymnastics. I'm thinking silver on the parallel bar in 2020.

On the boy's penultimate attempt I realized that his parents were videotaping his efforts. They were torn between the precociousness of the moment and their duties as the custodians of ushering into society a well-rounded, courteous person. They grow up so fast and those moments may never happen again. At least that's what they can tell the judge at his sentencing twenty years from now. I kid, i kid. I would've seriously been between the same rock and hard place. Especially given the boys climbing proficiency. Catch you teach and capture?

FATHER: Ok son, we need to get this in one take then go get a switch from the yard for your beating.

Ain't No Party Like a Dubai Party…

So After my show in Dubai I went to a night club in the Address Hotel in the Dubai Mall. It's apparently the largest mall in the world. The "est" suffix comes up a lot when speaking about Dubai. The root words in front of the "est" range in opinion and prespective.

I went to the Republique bar to catch up with my man Samer. He promotes the night. Yes, I catch up with people in Dubai. I get there to find Samer is spinning on the one and twos. Which at this point in history is the one and twos, and CD makes three, PC makes four and so on. He's a multi–media movement as much as he is a DJ. The place was packed. The lovelies were lovely and plentiful so the guys were happy and civil. I walk in and the crowd is completely jamming out to MJ's "Black Or White" with the accompanying video playing on the projection screens. Not the MJ song you would expect to hear at the peak of the night at a dance club but it was definitely a precursor for what was musically in store. Samer kept the party motivated with a mix of songs that felt like they came from a well rounded person's Ipod. "Black and Yellow" kept things lively but House of Pain's "Jump Around" was received almost as well as new cars from an Oprah audience. Great songs are timeless as everyone knew all the words and I was probably older than 85% of the crowd. Too old for the club? Again, I was supporting Samer.

The latest hits were met with game dance faces and the house/arab song set bought things to the brink. I bid Samer adieu as I had to get up early and attend to my work grid. I felt that Daft Punk's "One More Time" was a more than solid swan song. Not sure if Samer took my exit attempt as a challenge but just before I reached the door he kicked things in hyper gear by playing Jay Z's "Empire State of Mind." It was like a shot of adrenaline. Even the Philipino waiters joined in with head bobbing while reciting every line. I can't leave while dude who loves apple pies from Mcdonalds is playing. As "Empire State of Mind" wrapped up I was more than content and I turned to leave. Samer forced my hand again by playing Notorious BIG's "Hypnotize". (unh, unh, unh...Ha sicker than your average...) Damn you Samer! I've got a busy day tomorrow. Why won't you let me leave. I'm in the Middle East and Brooklyn is not only in the building, it's in the hearts of the people. Okay, now I can leave. But wait, says Samer thru his musical selection. He threw on Montell Jordan's "This is How we Do it" Okay this was now officially an intense cardio workout. I know each generation thinks their music is better but it's funny how he took it to the mid nineties to really set it off.

Then it got surreal. After Montell Jordan made the crowd go ape crap. Brian Adam's "Summer of 69" plays on the video screens. Every person was singing every word. I wonder what that says about different eras of music? Then he played Gun N Roses' "Sweet Child of Mine" and they took it to church. Most people, myself included, doing the patented Axle sway. I swayed out the door and heard the beginning of "Flashdance" as I hopped into a cab. Who knows where Samer ended up. Led Zeppelin? Motown? The people seemed down for whatever.

If I had to do it all over again, I would switch to music. It's crazy to have your thoughts said or sung to melody and enjoyed all the world over. Then again, I'm here doing comedy in Dubai so I guess I'm spreading my gospel. One room at a time.

Say it Don't Spray it

So I was hanging out in the Bayswater section of London. I consider it my old stomping grounds. So I thought, why not hang in Bayswater my last official night in London. I hopped into a Super Drug store to get some lozenges. The cold weather had finally got to me just as I was about to leave. My plan was to throw lozenges down my gullut and hope I didn't get too sick to watch 4 movies on my 12 hour flight home.

Cold-Eze are my lozenge of choice. The zinc tastes horrible but coats your throat and cuts the sickness time in half. Unfortunately this modern marvel of cold warfare has not made it's way to the UK. Regular menthol drops would have to do. As I stood in line the guy ahead of me made a purchase and the cashier tried to upsell him on a holiday perfume deal. CK One was on sale . I'm not much of a perfume person myself. I think regular bathing and Jergen's Original Scented lotion is all most people really need. You might catch me rocking Egyptian Musk if I recently made a trip to Venice Beach or Downtown Brooklyn but that's usually because I fell prey to a bean pie upsell.

The gentleman ahead of me declined the cologne offer but did spray copious amounts of the sample bottle on this neck and chest.

QSN: At what point does sampling become stealing?

Then this guy who I've never met before, sprayed me. And not just kinda in my vicinity. He literally sprayed into my open coat. Was he trying to tell me something?! My smell game is impeccable so I know I wasn't offending people in whiff shot. I think it goes back to my innate friendliness and approach–ability. The cashier informed him that he had actually sprayed me with the women's scent. The Spray

Sniper proceeded to spray me again with the Men's scent. I was too interested in the proceedings to stop him. I wanted to see just how far he would take it. Was this guy just completely unaware of social boundaries or was it something about me that empowered him? Would he have sprayed Mike Tyson if he was standing in line behind him?

The guy behind me in line seemed more put out than I was. His face formed into the shape of disbelief with a hint of happiness that he did not get sprayed. As oddly unlucky I was to get sprayed the sprayer was equally lucky that he sprayed me and not someone with no fondess for eccentricity.

Maybe this is why I like Bayswater. Maybe I'm one of Bayswater's own and with that comes random unannounced cologne spraying. I'm smelling what ya cooking Bayswater.

Going My Way?

So I recently wrote two blogs about a run-in on a bus between a passenger and the bus driver. This all went down in Birmingham, England. What I failed to share in either blog is that I got off the bus two towns too soon.

I went to a Subway and ordered a meatball something or other and asked for directions. The guy in line ahead of me told me I was way off and then offered to drive me there. I hopped in.

Then two days ago here in Johannesburg I was lugging my groceries back to my Bed and Breakfast when a guy who was at one of my shows pulled up and told me to hop in. I hopped in.

I've been the recipient of quite a few citizen taxi rides. I was once driven from a chicken spot called Mama's in rough area of Chicago to safer pastures.

(The tasty fried bird was well worth the voyage into the wrong side of town.)

I don't recommend car hopping to my readers. I have a good sense of people (knock on wood), a third eye if you will. I have also done some citizen taxiing myself.

I once drove a lady home to an area in LA called The Jungle. This is where the "I'm King Kong" scene of the movie Training Day was shot. And this was way back when it was still "The Jungle."

I don't hitchhike, but if you offer a hitch I might forgo my hike.

Okay, no one tell mother about this one.

Signore! Signora!

I was recently on the metro train in Rome. The one in Italy not New York. The Rome metro is awesome. Italy only has a few lines on their metro but the subway cars don't have doors at either end in between. Just a circle that each car can swivel on. So if the train is going straight you can see unobstructed straight through from one end of the train to the other.

This makes for very easy movement from one subway car to the next. In New York you either have to walk in between the cars, hitched together by a very big bolt and 2-3 bank style stanchion ropes with a lot of slack preventing you from going overboard as long as you put absolutely no weight on them. The other option is to wait until the train stops and run from one car to the other. Probably dozens of people each day do this and for some reason or other don't make it to the next car. Not only must they wait for the next train, they also must brunt the shame and ridicule of the stationary passengers riding by them saying "what an idiot" with their eyes and mouths.

The Rome metro setup is perfect for panhandlers. I was on the train all of 5 minutes before a very young girl of 11–14 years old came into the car, dropped to her knees and shrieked "Signore! Signora!...." I couldn't understand but my brain heard..."me-a so-a poor-a"...

She went to each person in the car with her hand out and the biggest, saddest eyes I've seen since this woman who used to come into the 24 hour Fitness I worked in without a valid membership and stare at me uncomfortably until I let her in.

I didn't give the girl money because I don't like pulling out any money in public. Especially in a place I don't know well with currency I don't know well.

No donation notwithstanding, I marveled at the girl's technique. I've seen my fair share of panhandling and this young girl has already honed her craft. I wish I had given her money. Not because I felt bad for her but for the entertainment value. As I got off the train I could vaguely hear her in the next car..."Signore! Signora!...."

Beg Like there's No One Watching

I recently wrote about a **girl panhandler on the Rome metro.** Her technique and style was so honed I figured I had seen the best Italy had to offer in the world of panhandling

Every once in a great while someone or thing comes along and revolutionizes a field. We call them game changers. The forward pass in football. The windows graphic user interface in computing, the juice box in beverage containment.

I think I witnessed the new standard of panhandling. It was like seeing Nirvana at a bar in Seattle in 1991 and instantly knowing that change is a comin'. A guy got on the metro reeking like fried dog pooh. Or at least what I imagine fried dog pooh would smell like. He had a low growl and was agape with very little in the way of saliva control. He then mumbled some garble. I'm sure even the native Italian speakers could not make out every word but we all got the gist. Then, he took out a harmonica and simply blew in and out as if it was a kazoo. After gracing us with the smell, speech and harmonica recital he produced a collection cup. It was either the funniest or saddest thing, depending on your level of cynicism. I don't think myself a cynic but I must to say I was squarely on team funny.

Here's the genius, some people pay because they feel sorry, others pay in hopes the donation will encourage him to leave their vicinity.

As if that wasn't entertaining enough another panhandler was also on the metro. An older man with an accordion. The accordion was spread open and ready to play when Grunt boy went into action. The accordion player, knowing he was bested, closed his accordion, put away his cup and got off the train. My guess is he went and got a job. Like a champion boxer who fights one fight too many I think he realized his time had passed. That, or he got off fuming at the utter lack of decency displayed by the harmonica blower... In my day there was a code to begging....

I figure the authenticity of the young begger was a 50/50 call. I chose to think it was a put on. I had so many questions for him: why the harmonica, do you have to wait 3 days to get funky or have you somehow infused the funk into your outfit, where can I get the best low-priced pizza...

Now we need to get the girl and harmonica dude on the same train for a beg off. Get the pay-per-view people on the phone.

When The Lights Go Down In The City

I was actually writing my blog about how England conserves energy when the lights in my bed & breakfast here in Johannesburg went out. I was scared at first. Every residence in Johannesburg is fenced in by electric wire. No electricity, no electric wires. My imagination combined with my inclination to worry, inherited from my mother, made me initially assume the worst. I made makeshift provisions for the ambush. I put on all my jackets, grabbed the biggest knife and a can of pork & beans. The beans were to be used for projectile weaponry not sustenance. Though I probably should have grabbed the can opener as a plan B. I actually have a long history of using cans to make my point. More on that in a later blog perhaps.

I was brought down from my

unnecessary and completely inadequate war preparation by the proprietor of the B&B knocking on my door to give me a candle. She said it was somewhat common and the lights would be back on in a jiffy. Los Angeles often has rolling blackouts in the summer so I should be used to it instead of going into Armageddon mode.

It was 830pm. I had 3 hours of charge left on my laptop but no internet. What if the lights never came back on? My laptop would became a snazzy paperweight. The lights were off for a little over an hour but it felt like a day. It was 9pm and I was considering going to bed. I can count on my hands how many times I went to bed before 2am last year. What did people do before electricity?! And don't say board games. You can't play quality Pictionary in shoddy oil lamp lighting.

The blackout reminded me how precarious and precious things are. It also reminded me that I must re-implement my project to hook my stationary bike up to a generator and harness my own energy...literally

The Yolks on Me

It's hard to eat healthy in places outside of the U.S. Well, that's if you're trying to make your body look like your favorite action hero. Jason Statham, I know you were dying to know. However it's a lot easier to eat healthy outside of the US if you're simply trying to be reasonably fit. The latter tidbit can be attributed to smaller portion size and occasional walking on the part of our foreign counterparts. Our mixture of gargantuan portions and lack of exercise of any body part other than our thumbs and index mouse clicking finger has super sized our nation.

Since the U.S. is about extremes, we juxtapose our collective girth with a sizeable contingent of health nuts. People who don't eat any bread, or refined sugar, and freak if anything that enters their oral cavity has any taste whatsoever. Surely, if there's taste, there's fat. Other places are just moderate. People eat decent portion sizes and go for walks. Done and done. No need to workout like Arnold or eat like Kate Moss.

This was highlighted when I asked the proprietor of my South African Bed & breakfast for egg whites. She had no idea what I was talking about. She's pushing 50 and doesn't know the term egg white! That's because they eat the whole egg. The idea of tossing half the egg is so foreign to them that it's laughable. And she's in great shape. I doubt that she hits a spin class tree times a week. The proprietor asked her daughter about these strange "egg whites" and the daughter's instant response was, "He must be American." So we're known as fat people who eat egg whites? We're a walking contradiction.

For extreme results, it takes extreme measures. But if you're moderate from the beginning you'll never need extreme results. Extremes make for good stories but moderation makes for a good life.

Good Fortune

I hope you caught my mention on the NBC nightly news. NBC happened to be in the Studio during an interview I did on a South African Radio Station. Shout out to KAYA Fm. I've been accused of having a horseshoe up my butt. You won't hear any argument from me. I am lucky and I'm the first to admit it. One day you're on a, dare I say, <u>World Tour</u>, albeit humble, and the next you're on NBC national news back in your home country on a story about the biggest sporting event in all of sports. One day I'll share more of my past but all this is very improbable if you knew my whole story. I'm not into the sob stories. I'd rather focus on the come-up. Anyhoo, Here's a link to the story and a rap about my good fortune.

<u>http://www.msnbc.msn.com/id/ 3032619/ns/nightly_news#37541224</u>

SERENDIPITY

Serendipity drips over me paint me
lucky
Right place at the right pace ain't it
lovely
When things fall in place, good grace
seems to touch me
my ace keeps me safe it's apparent that
he loves me
reparations for past situations float
above me
So I Stay in sunlight even night bounces
off me
my past seems distant but it's with me
like an anchor
so I'm close to shore even on a world
tour
no spiritual drift cause I'm aware of my
gifts
treat'em with care like it's December
26th
really no complaints it's my family that I
miss
never been a saint but the cameras say
I'm this
Humbly I accept piggy back on my

efforts
follow in my steps feelin' blessed is
what you left with
when those blessings come will you
recognize them
I count mine daily so I'm rarely
criticizing

Stop, Collaborate & Listen

So I'm in Johannesburg, South Africa with my good friend David Kau. We're at his house watching "South Africa's Got Talent." I never watch these kind of shows but when in Jo-Burg...Plus I was tired and jet lagged so a mind numbing talent show was probably just what my brain needed. I was willing to roll the dice on the impact on my soul.

Just when I thought my soul would cry one prolonged tear, a commercial came on that rejuvenated not only my soul but my mind and body as well. For years American stars have been secretly dipping over to Europe or Asia and pushing products for the man. And why not? I know I would sell toothpaste in the Netherlands if it meant I get to keep my house and not become a cast member of the Surreal Life.

So I perked up when a Castle Light

commercial came on pushing their new Ice beer and Vanilla Ice appeared on the screen dancing and rapping Ice Ice Baby. The commercial was hilarious and I'm officially giving much props to Vanilla Ice and to South Africa for getting the joke and letting Vanilla Ice get in on the joke.

If you want people to laugh with you and not at you then you simply have to join them in the laughter.

Ask yourself, would you rather work for UPS for 30 years or have one hit record and spend the rest of your life traveling the world performing that one song. Or better yet, ask a guy who works for UPS what he would rather do.

Castle Lite Vanilla Ice Commercial

even Louis Gossett Jr. got a piece

I Missed The Bus

I recently hopped on a city bus in Birmingham, England. The bus driver seemed like an okay enough chap when he confirmed that I was in fact on the right bus heading toward Shirley, England.
The driver drove all of 8 feet and stopped at a red light. I was still talking to him in fact when a woman knocked on the door trying to gain entry. The driver waved her off and pointed at the ground to indicate he was in a non-passenger pick-up zone. To the untrained eye he was still at the bus stop. Most people on the bus spied the woman with a "sucks to be you" look. That was all the compassion and confrontation 99% of the riders could muster up when from the middle of the bus we all heard…

RIDERWHOCARED: Bumma Clot.

Open da door now here.

I think most of us agreed with our high pitched Jamaican accent friend but far be it from us to tell the driver how to do his job. The driver mumbled something about double lines and not being able to open the doors in this magical zone just 8 feet from where the rest of us boarded. Problem averted right? Not exactly as the same passenger piped up again....

RIDERWHOCARED: Bumma, Open the damn door man!

I know you're probably thinking the same thing the driver was thinking... damn this is a long light! The driver finally drove off leaving the woman to stand at the empty bus stop and wait twenty five minutes for the next bus. At this point we were all looking back and forth from the rider to the driver like it was a long match point volley at Wimbledon. The rider had stamina and as the bus pulled away he piped up again..

RIDERWHOCARED: Bumma, you have no compassion. You've been a very naughty boy! A very naughty boy.

This is the point I had to bury my face in my arm to conceal and stifle my laughter. The rest of the bus was uncomfortable as you would expect being in the middle of this exchange but none of them seemed thrown by a grown man calling another grown man naughty. Maybe the rider was trying to shame the driver's inner child. Instead, he tickled my inner sophomoric frat boy. In the US naughty is reserved for people under age 10 or grown-ups with fetishes that go beyond the scope of this blog.

The mood calmed down and I got a hold of myself. But as the rider disembarked he said...

RIDERWHOCARED: Us poor people gotta stick together brudda. Ya tink the bus company cares about you? Welcome to da real World!

By the way the bus drivers in London and Birmingham are encased in protective plastic glass like a late night gas attendant. Maybe England goes hard.

Break, For Love

One minute you're at a bus stop in Birmingham, England enjoying the violin playing of a street musician. The next minute you're at a bus stop in Birmingham, England watching break dancers break to violin music and you don't care if the bus never comes. So, some breakers set up shop right next to a street musician and the result was a brilliant piece of audio–visual living street art. I'm not sure if the breakers and the violin player are a package but they should be. The blaring violin juxtaposed with the acrobatic feats better showcased the dancing than hip–hop would have. Hip Hop can be abrasive but the moments were fluid and smooth. At first what seemed like a contrast proved to be a parallel. Two forms of art that both take physical discipline and control coming together. Each making it easier to appreciate the other.

The best thing was that the dancers and the violinist, though definitely putting their talents on display, seemed wildly content with the act of doing regardless what onlookers may have thought. There's power in doing something for yourself, sans chest pounding. I almost envied the woman who **missed the bus**. Enjoy the clip.

<u>break dancing to the violin</u>

Innocent Til Printed Guilty

I recently drove a Cadillac Brougham from Oklahoma to Florida. Impressed? Did I mention it had no AC. Now you're impressed and confused and some of you may be hot and perturbed even thinking about traversing the stifling Bible Belt sans AC. A picnic it was not.

I use the term stifling to describe the weather conditions although I think the adjective would hold even in cool weather. A bathroom/snack break in Alabama introduced me to perhaps the best and worst thing I've seen this year. On the counter was a newspaper that reports on who's been arrested that week. The paper has no articles. Just mug shots with the crime they're charged with as captions.

The back of the "newspaper" had a full page of a before and after picture of a woman titled: "The Faces of Meth."

Needless to say the after picture looked like Gollum after an all night bender. I guess...Meth is her precious... As a tool to discourage meth use I would give it an 'A'. On the drawing pleasure from horrific sights that should be treated with a modicum of reverence lest open the reader up to bad vibes, I give it an 'F'.

Now I can enjoy a Hot Mess from time to time like everyone else. Train wrecks have high entertainment value. But they are also high on negative energy. A balance must be struck between pretending the ugly things in the world don't exist and reducing all misfortune and pain to trivial entertainment. My observation is that doing either extreme results in the wrong thing being perpetuated. Either because people, having had no exposure don't respect its power or, because overexposure and trivializing it makes people forget its power.

Arrest records are public information so this paper gets a free report, adds sensational graphics and makes money off it. I bought one to sift through and make sure it was what I thought it was.

That will be the 1st and last one that I purchase. How about innocent until proven guilty? Does this paper plaster all the people who are found innocent on future issues? Not likely. With over a thousand cable stations and the entire web do people need this form of entertainment? I say it's entertainment because who really <u>needs</u> to know everyone in their county who was arrested the week prior? They have a right to produce the paper though. I hope we exercise our right to not buy it.

Saddest thing: One of the mug shots is of a woman who seems made up. Like she was taking a head shot instead of a mug shot. I hope people aren't calling up their friends bragging about such a dubious distinction. I hope those arrested aren't making bail and buying

8 copies of the paper on the way home to show their friends. But nothing surprises me anymore.

I have deliberately left out the name of the newspaper.

FUNNY, CUZ IT'S TRUE

Let Me Spell Ya Something!

I've been joking on stage about how I'm "International." Much truth is said in jest, so I do travel abroad every now and again but I'm no better than all you local folks. I just have more frequent flyer miles. A fact not lost on my family.

When I get the call, family members get the miles. You can't have your miles and use them too. So, I had no qualms booking a last minute trip for my aunt who had to represent us at the funeral of a close family friend. The whole thing went fairly smoothly but it highlighted the different styles used by me and my aunt when booking a trip.

People who don't travel a lot approach the whole booking process with respect and deliberateness more fitting of a bomb diffusion. My aunt had to write everything down and I had to give every detail thrice. I on the other hand, often don't know what time my flight on the next day leaves. An excerpt of me on the phone with my aunt booking the trip:

ME: Okay you fly out of LaGuardia at 1pm with a connection in Philly
MY AUNT: Okay wait a minute…bear with me…That's LaGuardia…L–A–G–U–A–R–D–I–A. at 1pm with a connection in Philly…P–H–I–L–A–D–E–L–P–H–I–A. I spelled it right, right….

I held firm and kept breathing. Eventually we got through it. She had all the info and I had a few minutes to spare before my show. Of course Murphy reared his ugly head and rubbed my nose all in his "Law." I had to channel more calm when I got a call from my aunt at 5am telling me she needed to change the destination airport. This time we got a customer service rep on the phone. With me in Sacramento, my aunt in Queens and Satish in India, all on a conference call, we painstakingly changed her ticket.

Having Satish witness the madness somehow made it better for me. We would both have to listen while my aunt confirmed everything 3 times.

SATISH: Okay, you will now leave LaGuardia at 5pm and connect in Charlotte.
MY AUNT: Okay wait a minute…bear with me…That's LaGuardia…L–A–G–U–A–R–D–I–A . connecting in Charlotte… C–H–A–R–L–O–T–T–E. And what's the flight numbers? Wait a minute. F–L–I–G–H–T…

I think I heard Satish put in for his vacation while my aunt was spelling out Columbia, South Carolina. Or maybe what I heard was his will to live leave his body. You want to bring back all the help desk jobs from India? Have my aunt call over there more often.

Fix Your Face

I love rooting against the team of the guy who paints his face. Very few things bring me as much joy as a despondent painted face. It's the proper conclusion to a bad idea. Sometimes the painted guy's team wins which only fuels his inner frat boy. Because his team is doing well his fellow non-painted fans around him get caught up in the jubilation and the wrongness of applying semi-gloss to your face gets swept under the victory rug.

As with all things, losing sheds a light on what's wrong. Winning covers things up. A team can be undefeated all season and no one may say a word to the loud cheering life-size swatch who calls himself a fan. But upon said team losing the championship game it's awesome to see the tolerant mob turn into and angry one. All of a sudden there's no patience for the loud face painter. He's now a mockery of what could have been. A jackass making the agony of defeat more agonizing.

Painting your face is like taking a half court shot during a game. It's fine if it goes in but say hi to the dog house if you miss. Women don't paint their faces and if they do it's a little cute design on their cheek. This, I don't have a problem with and seeing a girl with a painted cheek crying because her team lost is actually very not cool...unless she's with the guy with the painted face.

The Cake That Took The Cake

On my 6th or maybe 7th birthday my mom made me a birthday cake. It was your typical, out of the box yellow cake with white frosting. My childhood friends were there, the Jackson Five blared in the background. I was ecstatic. Needless to say I was enjoying myself. Pun intended. I entertained those in attendance with my MJ (Pre-thriller moves), my James Brown and my Robot.

Then in a magical, historical, God inspired instant my mom had the idea to put jelly beans on top of the cake. She absolutely blew my mind. She pushed the realms of the whole time/ space continuum. It was at that very moment that I realized that anything was possible. She was thinking out the box long before it became stale corporate jargon. I really think God worked through my mother on that day.. It was like the first homo-erectus man who stood up for the first time, like Edison calling Watson or like MJ moon walking on Motown 25. All the kids were awestruck. Mouths so wide open in amazement you could have driven a Hess truck down our throats. It was so simple yet brilliant.

It still stands tall as my best birthday moment ever. My mom and I still talk about it. We were smart though. We never put jelly beans on a cake again. We knew we could never duplicate that moment. No, that moment still stands alone as the birthday my mom became immortal and, on a whim, put jelly beans on my cake. Like the night Jordan dropped 63 on Bird.*

Thanks Ma!

* Jordan drops 63 on the Celtics
http://www.youtube.com/watch?v=ovt7UrA9djs

Split is A Four Letter Word

Ever go to A Birthday dinner at a restaurant with a group of folks? It's a given that the birthday girl won't pay and that the others will absorb her costs. This is always a risky venture for the non-drinker. There's always some big shot at the dinner, let's call him Chad, who keeps ordering rounds of rare, and for some reason alcoholic, unicorn sweat. And non-drinker is bummed because they ran out of virgin unicorn sweat. And how much does unicorn sweat cost!? Then Chad orders appetizers for the whole table. And everyone wants to go family style with dessert... Then the Bill comes....

And Big Shot Chad grabs the bill and starts calculating. Then he says the four words every non-drinker dreads..."Let's just split it!" The non-drinker doesn't know how to tactfully work into the bill conversation that he had no alcohol and fears being labeled cheap or petty. But they downed 3 bottles of 50 proof Unicorn sweat. That can't be cheap. Non-drinker, who may also be a finicky eater, also longs to remind his mates that he didn't even touch any of the Goat Brains appetizers that Big Shot Chad ordered and guaranteed everyone would love. But non-drinker bites his tongue so as not to rock the proverbial birthday boat.

But just then the group realizes that Todd's birthday was last week and they didn't celebrate. So now Todd is off the "will pay" list. And Suzy announces she's leaving for Buenos Aires for a year to study seismic activity.

Group: Ahhh!
Non-Drinker: (in his head) Damn!

Now she's off the pay list too and there's an earthquake happening in non-drinkers head.

Then after all that, Big Shot Chad forgot

his wallet but vows to get you guys back the next time. Now the only people left to pay this monstrosity of a bill is non-drinker and two notoriously low tippers.

And the Non-drinker screams to himself..."but all I had was a turkey club..."

*names changed to protect the guilty
**story exaggerated to garner sympathy for the innocent

Interview by the Vampire

I was in a quaint little mom and pop coffee shop the other day. I think it was called Starbucks. Have you heard of it? Anyhow, one of the workers, apparently a "Team Leader," sat at the table next to me with an applicant to conduct an interview. This Starbucks "Team Leader" was maybe seventeen years old and the woman he was interviewing was a grown ass woman probably in her mid-thirties. The "Team Leader" was trying to be professional but sounded clunky and awkward, like a person doing a testimonial on a cheap law firm commercial. He asked her about times in her life she had to overcome adversity and blah blah blah. Yeah, she's going through it right now being interviewed by a boy whose voice hasn't completely changed and having to smile and pretend this is a real interview. Just hire her and make her the manager already. I don't know this woman's back story but she must be super tolerant or really needed the job.

The only thing you should have to know to get a job at Starbucks is a small is a tall.

I'm Cool Like That

Sometimes things go out of style for no good reason. There's a general consensus that said thing is pretty rad ... and then one day, with no official meeting or memo even, we kinda all agree that said thing is out. And it simply vanishes without anyone even acknowledging it happened. Kind of like the younger sister on the show

Family Matters. One show they had a little sister and the next they didn't. They didn't kill her off or send her to live with a relative. No explanation at all was given. They just stopped having a sister. Orwellian indeed.* I call it the Digable Planets Syndrome**. We have lost some very useful things and people to this syndrome.To counter this unfair tossing away of things, I'm starting a campaign to bring things back that really never should have been exiled in the first place.

First up:
The four color pen! What a useful and awesome device. Four colors in one pen!! In fifth grade we all agreed that the four color pen was the key to unlocking our potential. The organizational implications were endless. And we all had a system. What was yours? Blue for math? Red for science? Or maybe you drew your color lines on time of day. Blue on Monday? Green on Wednesday? The sky

was the limit . You and your 4 in 1 pen were going to change the world. But while you were dreaming, life was happening. We got PDA's. We started dating. We stopped passing notes with heart dotted I's. All of a sudden we felt silly having a fat pen in our hands in public.

QSN: Either they made the four color pen smaller or my hands got a lot bigger. As a kid I remember having to switch hands or use one hand to guide the other. But now I can write with the pen sans hand cramps.

My friends, the four color pen is back. And it's not just for wide eyed kids anymore. I'm in a coffee shop right now proudly sporting my ink quartet. They still sell them at Staples and Office Depot. Grab one for yourself and one for the little ones in your life. This pen will change my life... if I could only remember what my system is.

ME: Was black for new jokes or blog ideas? Green is my things to do list... no...blue is my things to do list and green is movies to add to my Netflix queue...maybe I'll just use red for everything...

*Orwellian – refers to the world George Orwell created in his book 1984. Big brother was watching and could make people not only disappear but also erase them from history.

**Digable Planets – 90's hip–hop outfit. That splashed on the scene with their hit "Cool Like That." A ridiculously phat track but shortly after that we stopped messing with them. Maybe we can bring them back once we get the four color pen up on its legs.

QSN: Quick Side Note

Sonic Whisper

I am not a fan of whispering. In most cases talking regular in a low volume will accomplish the same thing as a breathy whisper. Whispering, at least the way most people do it, is unnecessary and in most cases insincere. It's a person's way of letting you know they are being quite instead of them just being quiet.

The whisper technique you hear most people employ seems to be borrowed from the stage whisper where the actors needed to let the audience hear them but at the same time convey to the audience that although the audience could hear them somehow the actor 3 feet away from them couldn't hear them. To accomplish this, actors had to speak breathy but loudly. So you see using this style of whisper is counter to being quiet. It's actually much louder. It was designed to be louder. I think deep down people go with the breathy loud whisper to feel special about having a secret or to be absolved from talking in a situation where talking is frowned upon… It's okay that I talk during this moment of silence because I'm using my husky whisper voice…

On top of it all whispering is ineffective and hard to understand. Back in my novice days of engaging in coitus, I used to employ the whisper technique. In your mind it makes everything special and heated but in reality it makes everything awkward. Being asked, "Can you repeat that?" over and over is frustrating in any situation. But hearing it during intimacy can be demoralizing. I finally dropped the whispering business when one young lady kept doing the exact opposite of everything I said. It finally hit me that she didn't hear anything I said. She basically felt hot air against her ear and adlibbed the rest.*

Let's leave whispering to the Ghosts.

*This really did happen a very long time ago in a galaxy far far away

Parking Lot Pimpin'

A lyric from a current hit rap song goes like this: "Gotta fresh line-up game, fresh pair of kicks, about to have the parking lot on smash…"

For the rap lingo challenged here's a translation: "I just got a very nice looking haircut where the delimitation between my hair and forehead (ie, my "line-up") is very sharp and neat looking.I have on a new pair of sneakers, probably Nike Air force Ones or some customized pair not available to the public. And finally, I'm going to be the best looking, alpha male of the parking lot, so much in fact that I'll be the talk of the parking lot.

Parking lot? Talk about all dressed up with no where to go. Why are rappers obsessed with parking lots?I don't even think they're going inside.New Yorkers don't drive but when we do we try to limit our time in the parking lot to as little as possible.Parking lots are for fender benders and lazy car jackers.I understand that in other areas of the country, clubs are in open spaces attached to parking lots but hanging in the lot seems like you're not completing your mission.And if the parking lot jamboree happens after the club, well you just seem a bit desperate at that point.Like you couldn't close the deal inside and now you're waiting for stragglers.

Maybe rappers realized that not everyone would see them in VIP so now they've decided to stand where everyone has to pass.It's all about how many people you can make jealous and you get more bang for your buck in the parking lot.Hell, you may even be able to piss off a few people not going to the club.Make a guy who just got off work and is walking to the bus stop feel like crap. We call that a two-fer. What would make these rappers happy is if they made a club like a plane. Make everyone walk through VIP to get to the regular club section. Here's what you won't be having. Damn this Cristall is good.Waiter, another bottle please... and could you tell these plebs to stop looking at me. I think your section is back there...

No disrespect to Rick Ross or T-Pain.Both have tremendous talent and swagger.So much in fact that they've earned the right to go inside the club and leave the parking lot to all the under-aged, non dress code abiding derelicts.

Last time I checked the biggest boss was in a corner office, not the parking lot.

Abs-Solute Closet

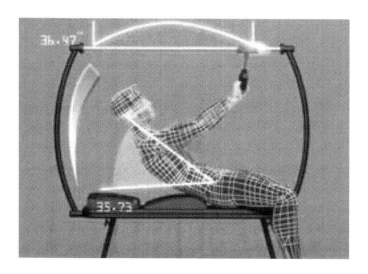

The latest revolutionary abs machine to hit late night paid programming is the Ab-Rail*. They seem to be getting closer to the truth with this one. It has a rod that goes straight across the length of the machine. It's like they're saying, "we know you're gonna hang clothes on it after a week, but with this machine you can really hang clothes on it."

They should make that a selling point.

207

When you give up, like you always do, like you must be doing right now to be up eating Rocky Road at 3am in the morning and wondering what magical machine is out there to help you get wash board abs. Well when you do give up, this time, all is not lost. This time, when the smoke of futility clears, you have a portable closet.

Just skip the middle man and go straight to Ikea.

QSN: The product is endorsed by Olympic Decathlon champion Dan O'Brien. I love it when they have world class athletes endorse these quick fix machines. Said athlete is saying, had this machine been around when I was training I might have had a childhood.

QSN: You know what else also works? ANYTHING! Just do something, do it over time and results will surely follow. You could do the Funky Chicken Dance for an hour a day and that combined with eating less would do the trick.

*http://www.abraildirect.com/
index.php?key=00117

Wear Sunscreen*

I play this game in my head where I have these answers for questions people haven't asked me yet. For instance, If I ever get to sit on the couch with Leno or Letterman I already know which funny, completely spontaneous ☺ , anecdotes I will tell them. I also have a witty come back for when Halle Berry asks me how come I'm such a good dancer.

To this end I've been working on a graduation speech that no one has asked me to deliver. I got some advice for that ass! What kind of person works on a commencement speech for absolutely no reason?! That would be me. I just don't want my speech to be something that evokes emotion but they forget what I said the very next week. I want them to be fifty and say…

FIFTY YR OLD: "This guy spoke at my

High School graduation and my life has been smooth sailing ever since!"

or maybe

RECENT HIGH SCHOOL GRAD: "Where was this guy when I started school?!..,That's it! I'm doing High School over. This time though I do it the DP way!"

The thing is to not make people too excited because they can't recreate that excitement back in normal life. You don't want them leaving your commencement speech needing constant motivating to be successful (See Oprah.) I just want to give them a few outline nuggets to make life manageable and to keep them in the game. I basically want people to live their lives as if they were the San Antonio Spurs.**

*Quote from a famous commencement speech that swept across the internet.

People thought it was by Kurt Vonnegut but it actually wasn't. Check the link.
http://www.wesselenyi.com/speech.htm

**The Spurs are an NBA team that has won 4 Championships. And although some think they're boring they seem extremely well balanced and adjusted. They never fall too far behind so at the end of the game they always have a good chance of winning.
http://www.nba.com/spurs

God...Semi Colon, Dash, Closed Parenthesis

At any given moment there is what is happening versus what you notice is happening. I think there are several planes of existence happening around us at all times. A person operating at a high level of perception and observation has more of a chance of getting glimpses into the universe's magnificent order. They come in the form of things repeating themselves or odd coincidences. But if you blink you wouldn't notice them. I call it a God wink.

On the days I'm not too distracted by life, I notice such things. Like on my way to Fresno, talking on my mobile phone, I mentioned I was meeting the other comics at a restaurant called Palominos and just then, at that exact same moment, a car passed me with a little trailer hitched to it that had the word "Palomino" written on the back. Coincidence? I don't think so.

Or yesterday as I sat in Starbucks writing a blog about Dubai, a guy at the table next to me struck up a conversation with a couple and told them he was from Dubai (He did not see my blog.) What are the odds of being in Fresno writing about Dubai while next to a guy from Dubai?

I get this kind of stuff all the time. But maybe the biggest God Wink of my life was when I went to Africa for the first time. I had always called my maternal grandmother Gogo. Odd name, but even odder is the fact that I gave her that name when I was 1 years old and just learning how to talk. Perhaps I couldn't say Grandma. Whatever the case, the name stuck and eventually everyone called her Gogo. It wasn't until I went to Africa that I learned that Gogo is an exact translation for Grandmother in many languages throughout central and southern Africa. And it was not until I went there that I, or anyone in my family, knew that.

So what does it all mean? I suppose it's not for us to know exactly but I do feel like I'm on the right path when these things happen. I feel good when I notice these winks. I think it just means that at least on some days, I'm centered and grounded enough to catch the universe's playful gestures

Wiki-Impede-Dia

So I figured I would make myself a Wikipedia entry. For an internet encyclopedia, for the people by the people, with everything under the Sun in it, I figured I could have a listing. Since…I am under the Sun.

I'm not completely familiar with the Wikipedia verbiage or format but I made a preliminary page. I listed only facts and maybe put a PR spin on it but I had no untruths. My page was up for all of 5 minutes before another user deleted it. Their reason for deleting me was: you can't use Wikipedia to self promote. Self promote?! Do people go to Wikipedia to book bands and comics? A person can only find me on Wikipedia if they are searching for me so how is that promotion when to find me they have to already know me and want to find me?!

So I sent that user a message pleading

my case and re-uploaded my page. Not 2 minutes went by before another user deleted it again. Then not another 5 minutes went by before a third user blocked me from doing anything. I felt like I was on the bottom of a nerd pile-on.

Here's what the second user, IceColdBeer had to say about it:

Hi Dwayne, I noticed you don't think your page should be deleted. There are a few reasons why it should be:
1. Wikipedia has a more-or-less strict policy about <u>notability</u> of article subjects. A quick Google search suggests that you <u>might</u> be notable, though there are lots of people who appear on TV who aren't.
2. Wikipedia has an absolutely strict policy about <u>not being used to promote yourself</u>
3. Wikipedia also has a fairly strict policy about <u>conflicts of interest</u>. Given that we require neutral

assessments of <u>notability</u>, as well as clearly-referenced <u>reliable sources</u>, you are not in a position to be able to accurately assess whether or not you are notable. If someone does write an article about you, you are welcome to <u>comment</u> on it, subject to our policies on <u>biographies of living persons</u>, as well as the information found <u>here</u>.

Oh and I forgot to mention that when I went to make my page, someone else who I don't even know had already made a page for me...and, for reasons unknown, that page had already been deleted. Not sure why but that was a neutral party. Everything I listed, my various appearances, was true and easily provable.

I deal with way more rejection and disappointment than the Wikipedia lot can dish out. I just don't appreciate the way they handled it. Deleting me before contacting me, blocking me. There are C level porn stars that have Wikipedia

entries. And I'm already on Wikipedia on a Comedy Central page. Fine, I'm not famous enough to be on Wikipedia according to the Wikipedia police. Worst things have happen. But those library nerds really let me down.
It wasn't done by committee just some guys who have some grand Wiki status. These are the proverbial gym teachers of cyberspace, wielding their one power with reckless abandon.

So to Realkyhick, IceColdBeer, Blueboy96 take your Wikipedia and stuff it. I still believe in the goodness and value of Wikipedia but those three can eat a Richard.

You can't fight city hall or Wikipedia.

Blame Canada

I'm in Starbucks at the Montreal Airport waiting for my chai latte (The Drink of Champions). The barista puts a drink down and announces "Latte." Now, I know the difference between a latte and a chai latte, but no one claims the latte and our barista seems unsure of herself. She inspects the side of the cup to confirm the drink waiting to be claimed is indeed a latte. So I very calmly ask "Is that a chai latte?", "No."

Okay, no worries, just trying to help out. Still, the latte remains unclaimed. Then, another woman waiting for a drink says "With a shot of Vanilla Hazelnut?", "No."

No problem. The woman was just trying to help. Right. We have hours before our plane leaves so clearly

there's no need for us to be snappy. Both inquiries were done in the spirit of being helpful and cooperative. The barista apparently felt a need to calm things down. She says "Please...just... Just...listen...this is a latte!" Finally, the owner of the latte makes herself known. Then the barista turns to me and in a very rude and condescending tone as if talking to someone who just learned English the day before says: "THIS....IS... YOUR...CHAI...LATTE"
What irked me the most is she was the only one remotely bothered. I wanted a referee to throw a flag or something. Like "We have a false 'calm down' on Ms. Rude. Which is actually 10 times more obnoxious. That's a 15 yard penalty. 2nd down."

In the end, you can levy the charge of rude and obnoxious on anyone by how you react. It would be like someone not stepping on your foot but you saying ouch at the top of your lungs. To onlookers, this guy is an inconsiderate jerk, but in reality, you're either a false accuser or you have some sensory issues and should really get that checked out.

Blame Canada, Again

I was recently denied entry into Canada. Well, technically my friend was but it meant neither of us could go enjoy Tim Horton's.* Why, you ask, were we denied? Not espionage or smuggling cigs. We were shut down because my buddy had a DUI almost two years ago. Apparently, DUI is a felony in Canada. Even though they drink like we do and I, the non drinker, was driving. So after a half hour wait in line, because we happen to be in captain 3rd degree's line, we drive up only to be bombarded with a flurry of silly questions, then directed inside where we got showered with more questions and ultimately shut down.

BORDER GUY: How long are you going to be in Canada?
ME: One day.
BORDER GUY: All the way from LA to Vancouver just for a day

ME: I was actually in Seattle for a comedy show

BORDER GUY: You came all the way to Seattle to see a comedy show?

ME: No, I came to Seattle to buy a ream of paper. I heard the Staples up here are a lot cheaper. Now, I'm going to Vancouver for post-its.

These border people obviously serve an important purpose but there is a little bit of Gym Teacher syndrome going on. Sometimes people with one specific power are drunker with it than people with a lot of power. Kind of A this little light of mine, I'm gonna let it shine all up in everybody's face type thing. Realistically, they can't put everyone through this rigmarole so they're either offering a false sense of security or are uncanny at picking only on people with issues. And since I personally know someone with DUI's who has been to Canada...a few times, I can safely bet it's not the latter. Had we simply drove up to a different booth, we would have banged up Route 99 to Vancouver banging Kardinal Offishall**. Luck of the draw.

The self righteousness was too much fore me to take. They told my homey he could try going to Canada again in 5 years if he proved he had rehabilitated himself. Oh Canada! Cut it out. You guys drink like fish up there. And for the record DUI is a business in the U.S., at least in California it is. I've seen field sobriety tests set up just over a hill 1 block from a strip of bars. Why not just before the hill? Why not place policemen in the street to scare people straight from driving under the influence? Because catching people generates income and preventing them doesn't.

Pull over everyone Canada and when you start having to turn away millions of dollars of business because at any given point you probably have at least one person in one of the cars in the question bays who has a DUI, maybe then you'll re-address this silly rule. Or why not expand it to stop all "bad" people. How about heartbreakers? You don't want people careless with others' feeling to be running amuck in your country. Or maybe people with halitosis. Surely, you could do without the air pollution. Or maybe just keep out all bad listeners.

I still love Canada but this is just one of those silly things I had to give them crap about. Or maybe I'm just mad because I was really looking forward to Tim Horton's.

*Tim Horton's is a fast food place mainly in Canada with very tasty sandwiches, soup, tea, croissants... It's kind of like Dunkin Donuts and Subways had a baby then gave it up for adoption and Panera Bread raised it.

**Kardinal Offishall – incredible rapper from Canada. It's the T-Dot! www.KardinalOffishall.com

Black People Can't dance

Okay now that I've got your attention let me explain the title of this blog. It's not that Black people can't dance. We can, especially yours truly. I just think this consensus that white people can't dance is wrong.

QSN: *As with any generalization, I realize that I'm painting with very broad strokes. But I'm painting an imprecise picture for affect.*

The theory shared by people, including many white people, is that white folks dance off beat. But it's all about framing. I say, they're not married to the beat. Which makes for a much more interesting artistic choice. Who wants 5,6,7,8 when they can watch a person immerse himself into a song on his own terms instead of the terms set forth by the unforgiving firm hand of the beat.

It's not about rhythm per say. It's about

being free and untethered. I can watch a baby walking for hours. It's a pure form of entertainment. Will the baby fall? Will she stop? Where will she go? What direction will she go in? She almost fell 5 times but kept going…the suspense is killing me. That's fun to watch because it's unpredictable and ever changing.

Cut to a white guy at a wedding going all out. Will he bump into another person? He's awfully close to the speaker wire? Is that beer he's dancing with full? That's more fun than say watching a boy band doing a polished dance number, right?

The moral is that whatever you do, if you have fun and are carefree while you do it, it'll probably be well received. The white guy who's dancing and appears to be in pain is painful to watch. But the guy loving life, albeit to the beat of a distant non-present drummer, is quite enjoyable.

Rapper's Delight Me

I'm completely addicted to watching freestyle rap battles on youtube. I'm talking hours of fun. I think rappers don't do anything anymore unless there's a camera pointing at them...

RAPPER: Yo this is MC Killa Fo Life and I'm just here fishing with my dad. You know what I'm saying? We using fly bait, ya heard!

I really suggest you go MC Battle surfing. For one, some of the lines are incredibly clever. But even if lyrics and razor sharp deliver are not your things, there's so much entertainment value in the whole process... The pre and post battle rhetoric, the homeboys in the background who don't talk or smile. What's a rapper without a posse? You can't expect the world to think you're hot if you can't find 5 guys on your block who think you're hot and are willing to spend hours standing behind you menacingly.

What I love the most is the odd mixture of raw aggression with utter nonchalance and lethargy. And the more menacing the guys behind you are, the more soft spoken and aloof you can be...that is until you start spitting*. It's a new brand of bravado where you're just too good to ever sweat about anything. I think the goal is to sound as inarticulate as possible before and after you prove how much of a wordsmith you are. You have to say "umm" a lot and look down a lot and seem almost annoyed to even have to be addressing your competitors. It's also preferable to be eating while you talk or doing a Rubik's cube or anything other than intently focusing on the subject you set up the camera to speak on.

I understand this mind set. I used to want to be good without people seeing me practice or work. For some reason we worship genius but we forget genius is 90% perspiration. Genius is fostered not born. I guess no one wants to reveal how hard they work, lest their competitors match their efforts. I wrote this entry in 2 minutes by the way...with one hand...while eating a Hot Pocket.

*Spitting – slang term for rapping.

Sorry I Said Sorry

Not to sound like I'm offering up a strength disguised as a weakness, but I say sorry way too much. The odd thing is, although I'm quick to please and quick to alleviate other's discomfort, I am definitely not afraid of confrontation. As a Brooklynite, confrontation is one of my major food groups. The Brooklyn food pyramid calls for more beef than most. So many of my "sorries" are born not out of fear or because I've wronged someone but out of a sense of compassion.

Cut to me in a Starbucks. I approached the coin operated door with what I thought was unwarranted trepidation. As I put my token in and turned the handle it became clear that my psychic abilities are in fact greater than null. I spied a middle aged rotund man sitting at the porcelain throne conducting business not suitable for a King. He shrieked as I instantly closed the door and offered up my most earnest of apologies through the door. As I gave my brain an ultimatum to forget what it had just saw, I also cursed it for not taking heed to my mild clairvoyance and knocking first. The man in the bathroom let out a "what the *expletive!*" In between multiple apologies, and bleaching my short term memory I casually suggested, through the still unlocked door, that he lock the door next time. His reply was that he did in fact lock it. Maybe a faulty lock was to blame?The entire ordeal took no more than 5 seconds. Of which 4.7 seconds were spent on apologies and explanations.

Another 5-10 minutes passed before he emerged from the bathroom. For safe measure and to let him know there were no hard feelings and more importantly, no judgment. I said sorry again. The jilted squatter walked pass me without any acknowledgement and with major attitude. I also felt some hint of aggression. As I brushed out my eyebrows in the mirror, some guy tried the bathroom door handle. I escaped the same fate as the jilted squatter before me because I had <u>locked the door</u>. Alas, the lock did work. I was already put off by the guy before me but now I was retroactively incensed. He forgets to lock the door and gives me attitude. Not to be rude but given what my eyes had to see, he should be the one apologizing to me.

I walked through the Starbucks looking to take back my sorry and offer my large friend an outlet for his misguided aggression if he felt like reverting back to behaving like a man. He had already left so I was left holding that hot potato of negative unjust energy.

This and incidents like it have prompted me to implement a policy of taking sorries back. I could just not say sorry but that's not my style and I don't want to take away people's chance to be magnanimous. So if I say sorry, especially where one wasn't even called for and you decide to take that time to dump your crap on me. Prepare to meet a guy from the projects in Brooklyn, New York. I wanted to channel the bad energy into the face of my bathroom nemesis but this blog will have to do.

Economic Stimulus

I was at the check out belt in a supermarket. There was a TV screen at the register advertising store deals and making a last minute push for customers' left over impulse buy money. A store ad came on suggesting people spend their economic stimulus tax refund on groceries. If you spend an extra 600 dollars on groceries, then you don't have extra money. That's catch up money not throw around money. Maybe they should call it an economic fix package. Economic stimulus suggests extra money that will help struggling businesses as well as the consumer. The supermarket chains are going to be fine. But a small mom and pop that sells glass unicorns, they need people to have extra disposable money. I know when my money is low the first thing I do is cut back my glass unicorn allotment.

Where's the stimulus if the money isn't spread around a bit? A person should be able to use an extra 600 dollars to take those krumping classes they always wanted to take.*

So is this the direction we're taking? Redefining prosperity and comfort right before our eyes. Changing the very definition we have been fed all these years. Now groceries are a bonus? What's next, we give our kids bed sheets for graduation? I'm not for over consumption but you can't take a zoo animal and release it into the wild and act like it's no big deal.

Unicorn anyone?

*Kurmping – Powerful, energetic form of hip hop dancing born on the streets of Los Angeles
http://youtube.com/watch?v=7GMNbZ8B1xA&feature=related

MORE CITY OF ANGELS

Take This Money!

I was at a taco truck in Los Angeles just around midnight wolfing down a tasty chicken taco when a man asked me for a dollar for the bus.   He was unkempt and smelled like he'd been hitting the sauce pretty hard...and I'm not talking about Ragu. He had a film on him. His dingy veneer looked as if it came from hard labor. Like maybe he worked in a mine. But we were in the Silver Lake section of Los Angeles where the only mining happening is Hipsters digging thru second hand clothes bins for T-shirts whose message once meant something to someone but now serve as bragging rights for people trying to thumb their nose at context.

The beggar seemed earnest which made it uncomfortable to say no. Even worse, I was scoffing down a taco and had a scarf looped around my neck. Here's a guy begging for a buck and I have on a snug scarf in 45 degree (brrr, but not really) whether. Whatever use he intended for the money was probably going to be more valuable to him than what I would have done with it. I just spent five dollars on tacos. No one with a warm home, a half full fridge and a cabinet loaded with nonperishables needs to stop and get a taco at midnight. Especially, if that person is sober like I was (drunk people, get your taco on!)

The former thought occurred to me as I crunched and gnawed. Me eating a taco is not a pretty sight. I eat with intensity. A stranger might mistake it for my first meal in a long long time. Basically, I become an action hero: This time, He's eating For Keeps!

I stopped chomping for a second and pulled out my spare change. I couldn't give him a dollar as I don't like pulling out paper money in case the solicitation is a ruse and it's really a two man job with the second man waiting to swoop in for my cold cash. Has Brooklyn made me not trusting?

I gave the man a handful of change and he proceeded to run across the street and hop on the bus. He actually used it for the bus! I didn't think it possible but my taco became even tastier as my beneficiary embarked on his journey. I just hope he hasn't worked out a "hop on the bus for a stop or two" scam with the bus drivers.

We Came, We Saw, We Kicked Glass

I was recently in a Tae-Bo class in LA. Well, technically it's called Drenched Cardio but it seems to have all the same moves as Tae-Bo. Plus, the proprietors are Billy Blanks'* brother and sister. The Drenched cardio guys get mad if you call it Tae-Bo. We settled on me calling it Drenched Cardio and simultaneously winking. I would add a nudge but Michael Blanks is 6'4'' and jacked...so, he might nudge back. I love how descriptive the name is. It's an intense cardio workout and you actually leave drenched...brilliant! I'm not writing this from a Coffee Shop; No, I'm in an unsellable screenplay manufacturing room.

QSN: I used to work in a place in downtown Brooklyn called for Goodness Steak. It was set up just like a Sizzler. They even took Sizzler coupons but managed to escape those pesky franchising fees.

But I digress. The Drenched Cardio class 😊 is always filled to the rim with people trying to stay fit. I'm sure that even if you just stood in the class and did nothing, the body heat alone would provide a moderate workout. So, we're doing squats with a kick, when I look up and see a girl doing her exercises outside on the street. She was just beyond the glass following our every move. Genius! She was cool, had all the room she needed and if she was really gangster, didn't even pay for the class. I'm thinking about taking up karate using this method. I'll just stand outside of a dojo and follow their moves. And when the sensei comes out I'll remind him that we live in a free country. It would be great if he tried using physical force and I used the moves he himself had unknowingly taught me to take him down. Then all his students would leave him and sign up for my karate classes which I would obviously teach in the park.

*Billy Blanks – creator of the Tae-Bo workout, a combination of Tae Kwon Do and boxing. Two forms of fighting merged to make a great workout but a completely useless form of self defense.

http://www.billyblanks.com/

QSN: Quick Side Note

Five, Six, Seven, Eight…

So I went to do a Drenched Cardio class aka Tae-Bo class. They don't like you to say Tae-Bo but it's many of the people from the old Tae-Bo class doing moves almost identical to the moves we did in Taebo with Billy Blank's brother Michael leading the class. A Tae-Bo class by any other name…

I knew it was a hip hop themed class but I thought that meant more hip hop music and maybe more hip-hop inspired kicks. In actuality it was more of a dance class. Like a learn a routine from scratch, move by move class. These can be fun but stopping to watch a new move every other minute isn't exactly an intense cardio workout and you definitely don't leave drenched. Maybe you leave empowered by having learned a new routine you can do at the next family reunion but not drenched.

As I'm known to eat M&M Peanuts at night right before bed or to down a bag of Gold Fish as I watch the 2am Sportscenter…I was definitely in the market for a workout of the drenched variety.

I was game though. Plus I kind of needed to baseline where I am in choreographed dancing because I've been toying with the idea of getting a crew together and giving MTV's America's Best Dance Crew a run.

That dream died in the Tae Bo studio. I can still cut a rug but organized group dancing seems to no longer be my thing. *Was it ever my thing?* I felt a bit of smugness from the quick learning regulars. But like I said I can still cut a rug. I was just rusty with the 5,6,7,8….. I was this close to challenging them to a krump off.

You can count and step but how strong is your core. Can you do a controlled seizure. Can you Harlem shake huh?! Can you look like a spider is crawling down your back on rhythm!?…well, I can!
me kinda krumping…kinda

Where Have All The Cowboys Gone

If chivalry is not dead, it's definitely on life support. Yesterday, while sitting in my favorite local Boba spot*, I saw a college aged baseball cap wearing guy with unwarranted confidence and formulaic swagger. You know the type.   They've learned that sticking your chest out and looking cool can get you by most of the time. That is, until you find yourself surrounded by people who respond to talent and character more than posturing. You may think I'm being hard on the young lad but my knee jerk assessment was soon confirmed.

He was with a girl. A tall modelesque creature with legs for days and a really pretty face. I could see that the guy was punching above his weight and maybe that was the reason for him over doing it. For men, when in doubt, be confident.   Women often confuse arrogance for confidence and being unconfident is a certain kiss of death. So I decided to give him a pass. Fake it til' you make it. Show no weakness, lest you lose your tall pretty drink of water. Then he proceeded to kill an ant with a sledge hammer. I'm saying he was too cool...he went too far...he...(just read on)

Apparently the kid had one stamp to go on his frequent buyer card and then he would be awarded a free drink for his devoted patronage. I'm thinking this guy scored. He can get the girl a fancy schmancy drink and not spend money set aside for his lab books.

Then came the "Oh no he didn't?!" moment. He asked the cashier if the lovely could buy herself a drink and if he could then take her stamp and use it to get himself a free drink. So, not only did he not but her a drink, he used her purchase to contribute to his "free" drink. The cashier was stunned. I Imagine the girl was stunned too but too caught off guard or polite to say anything in that moment. Or maybe the kid acting like a "Nickname for Richard" made him more appealing to her. Maybe he just earned 3 more dates by being an ass. Maybe she'll date him for months or years. Maybe they'll marry and have kids. Whatever the case when they split (yes, when not if!) she'll think back to the boba date and think to herself that she should've known.

I could tell by the body language that they weren't old friends. He proceeded to talk about everything with that air of self–

assurance that only someone with no self assurance can pull off.

I'm sure I've done my share of selfish things without even realizing it but setting the collective bar so low will eventually be bad for both genders. Malcolm X said you can judge a nation by how they treat they're women. America, can we buy our women boba tea? Or at least use our "free" tea on them. The world is watching.

So I Creep…Yeah…

Let's workout a little math/logic problem:

*Most women don't like creepy men

*Most men, even good ones, can become creepy around scantily clad women

*Many women dress scantily clad given the opportunity (ie Halloween and bars)

Therefore:

*Many women may want guys to not be creepy but are unwilling to help them in that endeavor.

Everyday, especially in Southern California, is an epic battle between men and women. The women seem to secretly want guys to be creepy so they can say…"What a creep!" And guys want to get away with some modicum of creepy behavior without being labeled a creep.

I was hanging with a wily veteran who has actually mastered the art of using reflections to people watch without being caught. I'm talking shiny cars, mirrors in bars, a big soup spoon....That's a lot of skill and cunning just to get a second look at a beautiful woman who has on an outfit that dares you not to look.

QSN: I've always thought it odd that people wear less clothing to beaches and pools than they sleep in. A wife in a nighty will put on a robe when her husband's friends come over but will wear a bikini, which reveals more than her nighty, in front of those same friends if they're at the beach. I wonder what takes precedent if you live in a beach house? Let no one say that i'm afraid to ask the tough questions.

The bottom line is we all want attention. Some people need oodles others just a smidgen but no one can get by with none. The problem is our current setup can lead to regular, respectful men with a healthy and innate appreciation of women getting bunched in with real life creeps. Okay, you caught me taking a second look but that's not going to get me on Dateline and I'm sure even Chris Hansen says...Damn Ma!... every now and again.

I have no problems with a woman in an itsy bitsy tinnie winnie yellow polka dot bikini but do you also need glitter and some push up device to go along with it?

If a rich man doesn't want a gold digger than it would behoove him not to flash his riches.
Even better, he should get a job at McDowells

Push The Little Pastries and Make'em Come up

I was recently in a Coffee Bean in Beverly Hills. Coffee Bean is the 2nd largest Coffee shop chain in Los Angeles. Of course Starbucks is the biggest. Coffee Bean is the runner up to Starbucks much like Sandisk is the 2nd top mp3 player after The Ipod. What's Sandisk?...Exactly.*

But I felt good being in number 2 on this day as the Coffee Bean was directly across from a Starbucks. Shunning a corporate giant for a smaller corporate giant isn't exactly sticking it to the man but you have to start somewhere. Given the option at least I went with what was closer to Mom and Pop on the Mom and Pop–Evil corporate giant continuum. For the record Coffee Bean has better tea than Starbucks. Starbucks has better food, mainly because Coffee Bean doesn't serve food. It's a push on the pastries.

QSN: Doesn't "Push on the Pastries" sound like the name of an Indie rock group? Eventually people would just call them POP and that would be coincidental but we would call it ironic.

I guess I'm all about the underdog as long as the underdog is directly across the street. A brilliant strategy when you think about it. Want to open a small independent coffee shop? Well, set up shop near Starbucks. Some traffic will be diverted your way out of pangs of guilt. Why be cliché when you can cross the street and be self righteously cliché? Others will head to get some indie brew to avoid long lines and no place to sit. Either way you're siphoning off the man and championing small business.

Who knows Starbucks may even pay you off and give you more to scram than you would've made in business. Sure, that's the classic definition of selling out but…if a thousand Mom and Pops do this then… Well, I would like to say it would bring Starbucks to its knees but it's more likely that scones will go up 5 cents. (in Robot voice) …Resistance is futile, Just go to Starbucks sip on your frap and enjoy Norah Jones on the PA system…

A Home Where the Paparazzi Roam

I was recently in a **Coffee Bean on Beverly Blvd** in Los Angeles, much to the imaginary chagrin of the Starbucks across the street. I was most likely youtube-ing rap beefs when a guy sat next to me and opened up a laptop with pictures of Serena Williams having lunch with a friend. Then, another sat on the other side of me and opened up a laptop with pictures of Serena Williams...eating lunch with a friend. Yes, I was the middle of a Paparazzi sandwich.

My general disdain for them and what they stand for couldn't completely quash my intrigue. Should I tap one on the shoulder? Maybe learn something about them that could humanize them in my mind. Or learn something about their work that might sway my thoughts.

QSN: I've hung out at the intersection of Beverly and Robertson in Beverly Hills before and it seems that every time I go there, there is a star sighting or two and paparazzi present to capture it. Which begs the question: Do people go there to be seen or does paparazzi go there because they know stars tend to hang there? Seems to me any star hell bent on not being seen would avoid this street like the plague. I smell complicity.

To chat not or to chat with paparazzi, that was the question. One seemed really involved with his work. To the point of it seeming like he was trying to convey self-importance but didn't feel quite justified to stand up and scream, "I'm important!" So his deliberately furrowed brow would have to do the screaming for him. The other got on his phone and spoke so loudly I wondered if he understood the technology in his hand at all. So he too was self-important...or hard of hearing. I'm perfectly okay with public phone talking in most scenarios as long as the volume and topic of conversation is agreeable.

In the end I decided against saying anything to either. It's best I not talk to people I already don't like. It wouldn't have taken much for me to treat either like a piñata if they tried to get brand new*. I may have passed up an opportunity to be pleasantly surprised but I also avoided a night in jail. Of course, ironically, maybe be pouncing on paparazzi would've made me paparazzi worthy. I think I made the right choice. And no, I wasn't there to be seen. I was there for a Nissan Commercial I didn't get.

*Brand New: being disrespectful, condescending or aloof because of a new acquisition, new station in life or the thought that the person you're talking to is beneath you and won't run up in your mouth.

Poland Spring

So I'm in the Bucks rocking a Triple 5 Soul Shirt. Triple 5 Soul makes quintessential hip hip-hop/ skateboard wear. Although now I have moved on to Teruo gear. My Compliments Per Wear (CPW) are about 40% higher with Teruo shirts then they are with 555 Soul shirts.

So when I'm in a 555 shirt, I'm usually playing the cut (*Ebonics for Incognito*). So imagine my surprised when on my way to the bathroom, I felt an arm reach out and grab me. I looked down and saw a very meaty forearm holding my arm. I looked up to see an older gentleman that I instantly recognized as someone who could kick my ass. Funny how, as a man, there's some guys you are willing to mix it up with and then there's others that you just know would destroy you… even if they are sixty two.

The gentleman spoke and instantly confirmed my suspicion. He asked me if I was from Poland. I knew those were Eastern block forearms. Is it me or do guys from Eastern Europe have bigger forearms then everybody else? I nervously laughed as I thought to myself….*Please don't beat me up Mr. Eastern Block who's been through more than I could imagine and could probably kill me with one hand…*

He laughed and told me I had a Polish flag on my shirt. Unreal that I've had the shirt for 5 years and never knew that. He seemed happy about me wearing the Polish flag. We shared a chuckle and I exhaled.

Crazy how we reduce everything to Pop Culture. You show me a great cause or a revolution and I'll show you a funny bumper sticker or cool T-Shirt. Poland has a rich history and I'm walking around unknowingly wearing her flag. This reminds me of the time I went to Israel and the girl I was dating at the time begged me not to wear my camouflage pants. I acquiesced thinking all along it was an unnecessary precaution. My run in with the Polish ex-pro wrestler now has me thinking it's a good idea to wear non-affiliated clothing when traveling.

I need to research the rest of the patches on my triple 5 Soul shirt. This would not have happened if I was wearing the new hotness aka one of my Teruo shirts.

Flying Carpet

I'm going to an event tonight where I'm one of the invited Red Carpet guests. It's a party for the Junior membership of the Hollywood Radio and Television Society. I've always been fascinated by how people react to Red Carpets. Take a disheveled hipster walking down the street and no one thinks much of it. Put that same guy on a red carpet and now he's someone people need to know.

I love to watch onlookers try to figure out who people are on the red carpet.

ONLOOKER1: *Who's that?*
ONLOOKER2: *I don't know but let's get his autograph.*

Onlookers just assume that it's their

bad they don't recognize the folks cheesing for the camera. See someone you have never laid eyes on walking on a red carpet and clearly you need to get out more. The best is when someone comes up to me and asks,

INQUIRER: *Are you somebody?*

Are they inquiring into my popularity or is this a philosophical question tackling the of existence of mankind.

ME: *I walk on red carpets, therefore I am?*

If this kind of thing becomes common place for me I may start giving my red carpet passes to my cousins from Brooklyn (the ones who never left Brooklyn) and let them go in my stead. Of course I would post up near by with a ginger ale and bag of pretzels watching people try to place the guy diddy boppin with a Yankee hat on and a toothpick in his mouth.

PRESS: *And what do you do?*
MY COUSIN: *I do me son…Fix ya face!*

Ginger ale pretzels and a fish out of water…What more could you ask for?

The Great Outback Mountain

I was recently sitting on a bench in Hermosa Beach, CA. drinking a chai latte and people watching in between shows at the Comedy and Magic Club. Hermosa is a beach town and also a party spot on the weekend. So, between the beach dwellers and party people, we're talking prime people watching. So I'm going through the mental utterances we all do when people watching: "What's the deal with that shirt?", "How did she get into that?", "No way those two are a couple", "The jogging doesn't seem to be helping that guy one bit." Just good old people watching with the directors comments thrown in, when very suddenly the watcher became the watched.

A group of people walked passed me. Singing, what seemed to be alcohol induced ditties. One guy, with an Australian accent said, "Howdy mate", then kissed me on the cheek. It happened so fast that I didn't have time to give him the Heisman*. His friends corralled him and off they went. The whole incident was no more than 5 seconds. Should I feel violated or appreciated? Was I a victim of a gay freebie or just some stranger male bonding? Is that the Australian way? Or, maybe I'm so friendly and approachable that this guy had to come over and pretend we just won the Super Bowl**. Or maybe he had a very severe case of beer goggles. But he did say mate so he knew I wasn't a Sally. It wasn't the Chai, so don't go there. It's not like my Starbucks cup said "Chai Latte" on it.

I think it's time for me to start wearing my Du-rag again.

* Heisman: To stiff arm. To thwart off with an extended arm, usually to the face. Kind of like speak to the hand but with actual contact. Based on the Heisman trophy statue in college football.

**Superbowl: Only time it's acceptable for 2 straight men to kiss each other is when they themselves have just won the Super Bowl.

Root, Root Root For The Away Team

I recently went to see my beloved Yankees play the Dodgers in Dodger Stadium. I like the Dodgers but I love the Yankees. The Dodgers pulled a fast one and only offered the Yankee tickets as a part of a package. To see the one game I really cared about I had to buy tickets to 14 games. I only felt slightly manipulated as I love going to baseball games.

So, wanting to see the Yankees precipitated buying tickets to 14 games which precipitated buying bleacher tickets which precipitated me fearing for my life when I wore my Yankees hat to said bleachers. The egotistic, nonsensical New Yorker in me thought that Dodger Stadium would be completely overtaken by

Yankee fans. Like it would basically be a Yankee home game that just happened to be taking place 3,000 miles away from New York. Maybe the 1st baseline was overrun with Yankee Blue but the bleachers offered no safe haven for Yankee faithfuls. There was just enough Yankee fans in the bleachers to make noise, band together and get completely drowned out by the bleacher Dodger rowdies. Sometimes having a small contingent is worse than having none at all. With no one to help you have no options but a small contingent may give you just enough confidence to engage in an un-winnable war. Did I just channel Sun Tsu?

LA fans are notoriously docile. I've out cheered my whole section at Laker games. Even other parts of Dodger Stadium are littered with hummus eating fans who arrive in the 3rd inning and leave after the 7th. The bleachers can be equally disengaged with the game but they replace game watching with booing, threats and occasional violence. For 9 innings straight, every Yankee fan that stood up or clapped was met with a chorus of boos and profanities.

So the Dodger fans gave us crap the whole game. What could we do but jar back? We're New Yorkers after all. As Mariano Rivera came in to save the game for the Yankees. I started to think a Yankee win may be be a Dwayne loss. I escaped unscathed but I may have to spring for better tickets next year. I'm a man of the people but maybe I can't sit with them at baseball games.

It's Better to Give

I'm not sure if I meet more odd characters than most people or if I'm just more acutely aware of my encounters with them.

I was recently in my home away from home. You might know it as Starbucks.

QSN: For the record I do patronize local mom and pop coffee shops and, in Southern California you might see me sipping on Milk Tea in your local Boba Tea house. The ubiquitousness of Starbucks and the never fail wi-fi forces my hand and sometimes makes the caffeinated Giant a must use establishment. Either that or work from home. And home is where the TV is. For the people still not with me, I ask you…why don't you find a mom and pop social networking page and get your Farmville on there?…I thought so.

Back to the 'Bucks. I was minding my

business trying to get through my emails as Cat Stevens' Greatest hits played on the PA system. As I involuntarily tapped my foot to "Morning Has Broken." An unkempt woman materialized before me asking me to watch her stuff. She pointed way across the room to a heap of worldly goods in overflowing garbage bags and sacks. There were at least 6 people much better positioned for watch out duty then I was. In fact, I had to change my seat so as to keep her portable kingdom in my field of view. I don't skimp on my look out responsibility. Especially when she went through the trouble of recruiting me personally for the job.

By the time she finished up in the bathroom "Morning Has Broken" had barely finished. Still, she was so appreciative of me looking after her things that she gave me 2 dollars. I tried to decline but she insisted that I take the money and buy a pastry. I humbly took the money. As I drove away from the Starbucks I saw that same woman trekking down the street with all those bags. It seemed she had no definitive destination in mind. I think a homeless person gave me 2 dollars. The coffee cake was bitter sweet.

Oldie But Goodie

I did a show in Hollywood last Saturday night and the comic before me was 92 years old. He started comedy when he was a wily 91.   He actually did very well and was quite astute at joke telling.

Right now you might be feeling bad about yourself. You should, but you should also be emboldened that the adage that it's never too late to be what you could've been is a real thing. I don't see Max selling out the Staples Center or starring in a buddy cop action comedy* any time soon but to have your health and wits about you enough to tell jokes at 92 is amazing.

A 92 year old gets the same crowd support that an 8 year old would get. The audience wants them to do well and is already impressed that they're even on the stage. It's adorable. The fact that Max hit every joke dead on was a very welcomed bonus.

What have we learned? For 1 comedy obviously keeps the mind sharp and secondly it's never too late. So pick up the phone and get the old band back together.

*QSN(Quick Side Note): If Max did star in an action buddy cop movie what would it be called?

- Old But Not Yeller
- Geriatric Tactics
- I'm Actually Too Old For This S@ $t!
- The Early Bird Special
- Stop! or I'll Poop

3 Dollar Salt

I recently went to see the movie Salt. The 3 dollar movie theater by my place is a real deal. The hot dogs are $1. If you can wait a month or two after a movie is released to see it, the $3 movie can be a very enjoyable MST (Money Saving Technique.) And get this, the matinées are $2. For 2 bucks the probability of any movie being a major disappointment is all but eradicated. 2 dollars buys you 4 stars in my book.

Now for 2 bucks, Salt was amazing. My 12 dollar movie review would be a smidgen more nit picky. It was a fun movie but Salt's plot would have to be in Salt water to keep afloat. It's just incredibly difficult to make high-tech action thrillers given the amount of technology available to the non-spy laymen walking the streets. These movies selectively disregard current technology as needed to keep the hero heroic.

The key is to have someone on the screen so attractive that viewers forget about all the contradictions. Of course I say "go see Salt!". Angelina Jolie on screen for 2 hours? I can give that a thumbs up without even seeing the movie. If movie producers were forced to put average looking people on screen, their jobs would be a lot lot harder. Don't believe me.? Just ask English movie producers. I'm kidding England. You know I love your fine ass England!

Back to Angelina….

You could pitch a movie about a woman who desperately wants to eat fried frog legs but can't find any toads in her sleepy town. She then meets a prince charming, kisses him and he turns into a frog. She's torn because she loves her prince but really craves fried frog legs. So, out of love for her prince she only eats his arm. Her undying love turns him back into a prince with one arm. It's cool though because they get to park in handicap spots and his arm never goes to sleep when she sleeps on his chest at night (because he doesn't have an arm) Of course, she'll have to get used to the left side of the bed…

And right before they tell you it's the dumbest thing they ever heard and call security to escort you out, you can mention that Angelina Jolie is attached and they will put the phone down, cut you a check and get the claymation department to start whipping up frog prototypes.

Better Suited

A few days ago I had to wear a suit and tie to a commercial audition. Commercial auditions provide an odd kind of escapism via adult dress-up. Where else but a commercial audition waiting room, on any given day, can one find adults dressed as: pirates, vikings, Santa Claus and/or his helpers?

The suit and tie is my favorite skin for a day. I was able to wear a suit I picked up in jolly old London. A European slim cut suit that I can only really pull off from certain angles. Those angles being the ones that don't show my high and sizeable caboose. To give you an idea if you haven't seen me before, I can reach my wallet from over my shoulder. *(picture it… there you got it)* So until I can lace my wardrobe out with custom everything I have to work the angles that work for me.

I kept the suit on for the rest of the day after I left the audition. It's a neat social study to see how people react to you in different garb. It's true everybody loves a sharp dressed man. I also get to occupy a space that could have been. Bend the time space continuum and get a glimpse of what 9-5 life would have been like had I stayed on that path. It was my own personal Halloween and I felt like trick-or-treating door to door for 401K plans, performance reviews and office football pools. I've never felt uncomfortable in a suit and I'm not the guy who unties his tie as soon as the work bell whistles. I'm also the guy who keeps the plastic on his watch and is writing this blog on a laptop that still has the sticker at the bottom of the keyboard telling potential buyers all the key features. (I've had this laptop for 6 months)

The commercial? For Xerox. I played an accountant who had to chew out the Michelin Tire man for some reports he owed me. How the Michelin guy ends up in a Xerox commercial can only be chalked up to cross-marketing. I'm not sure who came first the Michelin guy or the Pillsbury doe guy. But whoever was first may want to have their lawyers place a call to the other. Fingers crossed that I get a call back.

Friends in Cosmic Places

Not to be competitive, but I would wager that, unless you're in a rock band or are a magician, that I know a smidge more odd characters than you. It just comes with the territory. It's always fun when an acquaintance or friend does something that catapults them unto the odd list or bumps them up higher in the list if they were already on it.

I recently dropped off a friend after a show who had long since held a solid spot on my list of odd people. A red-headed (but more orange), chain smoking comedy booker with a piercing nasally voice and equally piercing inter-personal skills. Still, we get along just fine. Although I questioned his being of this planet when I saw a long centipede looking bug in his hair a while back. The bug was the same burnt orange color that his hair is. He flicked it off when I brought it to his attention but it just took me back to Men in Black. Plus, I don't think he was sufficiently freaked out that a long slimy bug was in his hair. So for a long time I held a faint suspicion that my friend was not human and in fact just occupied a human shell to do business and blend in until his mother ship returns.

Over time I loosened my belief that my friend who books one-nighter comedy shows in Orange County is actually an under cover extra terrestrial. Why travel across the vast galaxy to book bar shows? Although that would be a pretty convincing cover. So I dropped my friend off recently and he requested I drop him off at a barely lit Los Angeles street corner at 1am with no signs of people, residences or to put it short...life. The alien theory is back in full effect. I think I dropped him off at his portal back to his ship. I Made a U-turn and old red was no where to be seen.

Of course he may simply not want me to know where he lives or maybe wanted to score some drugs before heading to bed but I'm sticking with the alien theory.

Stop The Violence

Last week I did a benefit show for Bryan Stow.
He's the San Francisco Giants fan who was
beaten into a coma at Dodger Stadium. The
show was actually organized by Philadelphia
people. This is all kinds of ironic as Philly fans
are widely regarded as the the most rowdy
fans in the nation. They threw batteries at
Santa Claus! (to be fair to Philly folks, I'm
pretty sure it wasn't THEE Santa Claus) Kudos
to the Philly fans who put the benefit together.
I suppose karma, like any debit/credit account,
can be balanced off bit by bit. Provided the
interest isn't compounded daily. Luckily for the
Philly fans a deed of this magnitude is akin to
paying way more than the minimun balance
and this feat does wonders for my perception
of Philly Nation. Dodger fans, you know you've
gone horribly astray when Philly fans are
telling you how to act.

I was honored to be there and as I waited for
my turn to provide laughs I scanned the room
and felt pretty good about mankind. I cherish
those moments. Sad that those type of
moments are becoming more and more rare. I
have to store flashes of humans acting
humane like a cactus does water. So later,

when consideration and empathy are no where to be found, I can draw from a past act of kindness to give my inner hope sustenance.

I half jokingly tell people that I am a Jedi. My midi-Cholorian levels are certainly high enough.* Since I wasn't recruited at a young age and because Star Wars is fiction, I can never officially be indoctrinated into the Jedi Order. That doesn't mean we can't borrow from their teachings.

I think most fighting and banging comes from fear. It's foolish pride and a fear to back down or look weak. When you take a step back and take a look at it with that in mind it makes a lot of people, thought of as tough, seem quite weak.

Fear is the path to the dark side. Fear leads to anger. Anger leads to hate. Hate leads to suffering. So let's call all these tough guys what they really are, scaredy cats. Let's let how well we treat people define us. Not how bad ass we are.

Get well Bryan.

http://support4bryanstow.com/

* http://starwars.wikia.com/wiki/Midi-chlorian

MORE SHORTIES

Red Means Go

Shout out to Mr. Tae, our driver in Korea. He got us all around Korea safe and sound. Although there were a few times I thought he forgot he was driving a passenger van and not playing a video game. In the world of Mr. Tae, "turn only" means "turn only if you can't cut off eight cars and get ahead of them." "Stop" means "stop if you feel like stopping; if not, hit the gas and hope that the other driver cares more about his car than you care about your passenger van." And a red light means "do you see any cops? No... then hold on!" Mr. Tae was the highlight for me, though. What a great guy, when he's not putting your life in jeopardy.

Mr. Tae also loves the super fast bullet trains. As we passed by them, he would always point them out. Sometimes with both hands.

Nice Shirt…Not!

I was recently at a comedy show. I said to another comic, "Nice show."
He thought I said "nice shirt" and began to thank me for the compliment. "You know I try." Another comic standing near by chimed in, adding, "You know he always dresses nice."

Here's the problem: I actually hate the way he dresses. I would normally be cool with giving a mistaken compliment, but now I'm adding fuel to his bad wardrobe fire. Maybe he was reconsidering his look and now I've given him the validation he needed to not only keep his wardrobe but step it up a notch with its awfulness.
"Thanks for the compliment man…I think I WILL buy that tie dyed blazer."
I wanted to say, "Remember when I said I like your shirt? Please put a 'do not' in front of the word like!"

Instead, I bit my tongue… hard.

Wuss For Dinner

This morning I happened to be standing near some guys unloading a truck in NYC. They were unloading pipes and other heavy looking stuff. They all sported tattoos, work gloves, and a" get it done" disposition. I felt a bit like a wuss as I stood there putting on lip balm. Mary Kay lip balm.

These worker guys probably eat lunch out of a black metal lunch box and don't even wash their hands before they eat. Of course they hold their sandwiches with one hand. Then when they get home, they ask their "old ladies" what's for dinner. Whatever they eat, there has to be enough Wonder Bread to sop up the last bit at the end. I'm writing this in a coffee shop and just finished eating a currant and apricot scone.

V.I. Please

I was at a commercial audition last week. There was a sign in one corner of the actor's waiting room that said "VIP Area". And I used the word "sign" loosely. Think Kate Moss in Rosie O'Donnell's bloomers. The "sign" was a ripped out sheet of loose leaf paper with "VIP AREA" written once in pink marker then doubled over in orange marker. We've taken this VIP thing way too far. First off, there is no VIP area at a commercial audition. It's not like Denzel is going to come audition to be in a commercial with the Aflac duck. And if he did, would the ad hoc VIP sign make him feel good about going from Academy Award winner to Guy #2 in a Cheez Whiz ad?

"King Kong ain't go nothing on me...but even King Kong loves Cheese Wiz. It's Mo Betta!"

Art of the Massage

I recently got a 12 dollar massage in the mall. I have to say it was on par with some 15 dollar massages I've had... I'm kidding... It was great and up there with the 50 dollar massages I treat myself to once a decade. Upside, you get to keep your clothes on. Downside, everyone in the mall sees you sitting in the goofy chair and making massage faces. I think the secret to a good massage is to not relieve the pain and tightness in the problem areas, but to make another area hurt much more, thus diverting your attention away from the problem you initially had.

"Your lower back is stiff, huh? Let me kick you in the neck..."

"Wow, I can hardly tell that my back hurts anymore! Thanks! Um... how much do you charge for neck braces?"

Wonder Woman – PHD

When I was a kid and wanted to stay up past my bedtime to watch Wonder Woman, my grandmother would always send me to bed and say, "Wonder Woman got her Education. You have to go to bed so you can wake up and get yours." My thoughts were always the same as I lay in bed, disappointed. "She's a super hero. She's not educated. And even if she is, she's not using it." If I were a super hero, could I then stay up? Dwayne has to go to bed, but Perko the Great Spoon Bender can stay up as long as he wants.

I recently saw an episode of Wonder Woman while on a cruise ship. Now I know why I had to go to bed. It had nothing to do with sleep. My grandma, my dear beloved Go–Go, was trying to save me from watching the worst show ever made. She didn't want my artistic tastebuds to be destroyed. Maybe as a youngin' you can't see it but that show was bad with a capital d. It was baD. I think the cruise ships show it to force people out of their rooms to enjoy the festivities. All you people with kids or younger siblings need to ask yourselves, "Should I really let them watch Flavor of Love?!" The answer would be nooooooo boyeeeeeeee.

I may be aging myself with the Wonder Woman reference, but maybe they were already in re-runs when I watched them. Maybe!

Q Tips Or Bust

My quest to be no frills across the board had ended. I give in. No more cheap Q-tips for me. Or should I say cotton on a stick as Q-Tip is a registered brand name. (see Vaseline) From this point on I will only use Q-Tip brand cotton swabs. My ears deserve it. All the others seem to use the legal minimum amount of cotton. While each Q-Tip swab has enough cotton on it to top off a medicine bottle. If I wanted to clean my ears with a stick I could use the chopsticks from Yoshinoya, a delicious Japanese fast food chain; or the tooth picks from TGIF's tasty club sandwich.* I'm still on the fence on what level of quality I need from my toilet paper.

*I hope the shameless plugs weren't too much but my blog needs corporate sponsorship. And free Yoshinoya, TGIF, and Q-Tips would push my life dangerously close to perfect. Keeping my fingers crossed.

It's Got To Be Funky

I was getting ready to go to my local coffee shop to "work."* I was feeling vainer than usual and I decided to steam out the major wrinkles in my shirt. Wrinkles neutralized, I slipped the shirt on. As my head came through the shirt I began to think: maybe I wore this already... on a hot day, and maybe on that hot day I wore no T-shirt or deodorant, and maybe on that t-shirt-less, non deodorant day I did some strenuous activity. The funk emanating from the shirt is what led me to have these suspicions.

Can you say "quandary" boys and girls? I had just put all that time into prepping the shirt plus I was running late for "work"*. What to do? There was a maple scone anxiously sitting in a glass window wondering about my whereabouts. I exaggerated before about the smell. The stench wasn't too bad, only suggestive at best. (Just a hint of rankness) Only someone all up in my peas and carrots could maybe smell something. But...I would know. I spritzed my pits with Fabreze. Which made it smell like a funky person was walking through a meadow of lilies. Not good. In the end I put on the shirt and proudly walked out into the world. Going out a little funky is very liberating. Your confidence takes a hit but you're way more courteous to people. I mean you can't be funky and ornery.

They didn't kick me out of the coffee shop or make me sit under the air vent, so I think it all worked out.

To Funkville and beyond!!!!

FYI: If you come to any of my shows, I promise to be newly showered in clothes off the rack or fresh out of the dryer. J

*Some of you reading this may do heavy lifting or crime fighting and I would feel silly calling what I do work compared to what you do. Thanks!

Knockin' on Heaven's Door

How many times is it acceptable to try to open a locked public bathroom?If there is no key and the door of a small coffee shop is locked, after a good college try, can't the person on the outside safely assume someone is in there? Why keep trying, shaking and assaulting the door? Or maybe this bathroom door has a weird quirk that requires you kick it in to gain entry.

Here's another neat trick. You could just knock. I will answer a knock. I'm not answering someone attacking the door like a mad man. Someone may be chasing you, or even worse Africanized Killer Bees may be hot on your trail. I'm not rushing my "process" so I can get bum rushed by a gang of angry Yellow Jackets. How do I know you're not after me? That you're not some enraged hyped up coffee fiend mad at me for taking the last cinnamon scone (it was delish btw). If you're not any of the above then chill out and wait until I'm done. Obnoxiously fiddling with the door will only make me take longer.

ME: (V.O.*) Boy that guy banging on the door for the last 5 minutes sure does want to get in...my toe nails need cutting...guess I'll undo my boots...but first...I stretch.

*Voice Over. Like in the movies when you hear what someone is thinking.

Key Change

I was at a coffee shop recently and no one could use the bathroom because someone had left the key, which was attached to a big ladle, in the locked bathroom. On one hand, it begs the question: how could you forget a big spoon you so clearly had with you on the way in? On the other hand, how often does one have to concern themselves with taking inventory of big, impractical, obnoxious key chains before they leave a bathroom? When will they learn that you can't idiot proof the world? Not that leaving a key in a bathroom makes you an idiot, per se.

If it's a practical solution that these mom and pop coffee shops seek, they should attach the key to some sort of elastic wristband. With the key around their wrists people could never forget the key in the bathroom. Of course they could take the key with them but at least the bathroom wouldn't be locked. An impractical, but I guarantee effective solution, would be to attach the key to a person. Upside, the key could never be locked in the bathroom or taken out of the store. I don't think I have to go into the downside. What would you pay the bathroom key attachment/person anyway?

Maybe we could recruit homeless guys to do it and work off tips. No need to thank me. Coming up with solutions to make the world a better place is its own reward.

It's been a dream/goal of mine for some time now to have an industrial toilet installed in my own bathroom. I like the look of the cold and reliable stainless steel pipes and handle. I think I would sleep better with the comfort of knowing that my toilet is damn near clog proof. I would even flush magazines every now and then just to bask in the glory of the power of my porcelain god. If I ever do get the high powered toilet I think I will require my visitors to take a bathroom key in with them... attached to a spatula key chain.

ME: Could you hurry up in there... these pancakes are ready to be flipped!

Let's Get Ready To Fumble

Watching non-boxers box may be the most fun a person can have. I recently watched Todd Bridges fight Vanilla Ice on youtube. You couldn't write a funnier scenario. The first thing you realize is how tiring boxing is. Thirty seconds in and they're both sucking up air like asthmatics doing wind sprints with burlap sacks tied to their backs.

But let's not forget the utter lack of any discernible technique. Half the time they aren't even facing each other and the back of head and ears get most of the punishment as the wild punches search for a home but come up short or long. The punches are like bad settlers who never get to where they intended but set up shop and declare success anyway.

Boxing is called a sweet science for a reason. And as great as it is to watch two precision boxers go at it, it's almost as much fun watching two plumbers throw erratic hay makers at each others' earlobes. Sometimes you want Fresh Spinach and Mozzarella Layered Between Sheets of Spinach Pasta, with a Zesty Basil Pesto and sometimes you want Velvetta and tomato sauce on an english muffin.

Watching civilians box is even a notch below makeshift pizza. Civilian boxing is like peanut butter and jelly on saltines. Really good but not good for you.

Classic battles:
<u>Vanilla Ice vs Todd Bridges</u>

<u>Screech vs Horse Shack(no fair. Horse shack is like 50)</u>

Push My Buttons

Surely it can't still be cool to push an unsuspecting person into a pool. You still see it in movies but with all the cell phones, flash drives and cameras in the world pushing someone in a pool could be the equivalent of taking all their worldly belongings. It's time for movies to stop portraying this kind of vandalism as harmless horse play. If you push me in a pool you better make sure I have none of my electronic gadgets on me because after I finish crying...that's your ass.

When I see this act being done in a movie or TV show I always think, how irresponsible of the producers to not make it clear that in this make believe world the pusher had already ensured that the pushee's iPhone was under his chair. Or at least show the pusher suffering a terrible fate for not checking first.

PUSHEE: My blackberry is soaked. I'ma call a coupla hard, pipe-hittin' bros, who'll go to work on you with a pair of pliers and a blow torch...

I suppose if you suppose your friends have jerk tendencies then you should make any body of water a no electronics or cashmere sweater zone.

No Gym? No Home?...No Excuse

Last week on Highland Blvd in Los Angeles, I saw a topless homeless guy pushing a shopping cart. To be fair, he may not have been homeless, but as he was at least a mile from a supermarket and his cart was filled with Hefty bags and clothes, I think it's a fair assumption. What separated him from most shirtless cart-pushing transients was the fact that he was cock-diesel. This guy looked like an action figure. And he wasn't just bulky, he was cut as well. He wasn't in Rocky IV shape but he was in Rocky III shape. Not too bad for a guy with no personal trainer. Unless of course he himself was a personal trainer before the bottom fell out. So... is he doing chin-ups and push-ups at the park in between panhandling? Should I feel a little bad that a homeless guy is in much better shape than me?

"I won't give you money, but I will buy you a protein bar!"

Sing Like No One is Watching

The second I turn the ignition in my car, it becomes a karaoke bar on wheels with me playing the role of the guy whose turn it always is. I have a good time driving and I'm sure the other drivers get a kick out of my antics.

My singing in the car days may be numbered though. Half vanity and half saving my voice has caused me to adopt a style of cupping one hand near my ear while I karaoke on the freeway. Which I'm sure looks like I'm on the phone from afar. For me it's the best way to tell if I'm on pitch. How will I explain to a cop that I wasn't on the phone, I just sing like I'm cutting an album?

ME: You see officer I was merely simulating a studio session...isolating my voice to ensure proper tone and vocal integrity...Have you ever seen the "We Are the World" Video? Uh sure, here's my license and registration...

I've tried not doing the ear cup but then I can't hear myself as well. Maybe I should enjoy the voices of the professional singers and rappers coming from my speakers. A novel idea indeed.

MORE BIG APPLE

Citizen's Arrest? In NYC?

I was recently on a subway platform in NYC and observed a sign telling people to report anything suspicious. Shortly after reading the sign, I saw a family from the Midwest on the platform. How do I know they were from the Midwest? They were wearing dockers, plaid shirts and fanny packs all around. I tackled them. I mean in New York City, they really stood out. No, no that's okay, no need to thank me. It's the least I could do. That'll teach them not to look at an unfolded subway map in clear view. Any self-respecting New Yorker knows you can only glance at the subway map. Not a "Where the hell am I going?" look but more of a "I know where I'm going, but I'm just verifying what I already know" look. Who knows what old Gladys and Tom were planning?

How Much is That Doggie in the Window

There's a guy on Lexington Ave and East 60th street in Manhattan. He's got a little dog and little cat, both in sweaters, on a box wrapped in the American flag. And the kicker is that he wants money. This fool puts a dog in a sweater and wants me to pay him for it. The pets were cute I can't deny that but there were no discernible skills. What's next? A guy wants money for brushing his teeth with his non-dominant hand? "Look, that guy is clearly right handed, yet is brushing with his left... where's my money clip?!"

To be fair to this guy, maybe before he left home, the cat and dog were jumping around singing "Hello my baby, hello my darling...."

King of Leon

I am a fan of show business as much as I am a content provider for said show business. I can't keep up with reality stars though. I stay clear of oxymorons not in the food category.

So I'm transformed into a typical fan when I encounter a famous person. It doesn't even occur to me that I am sort of in the same business and to approach the matter as a peer to peer encounter. I've had guys come up to me who once said the general announcements one Sunday in church and think that qualifies them to talk shop with me about comedy. As amused as I am by these types, the fact that they once spoke in front of more than 10 people isn't good reason for us to share stories from the "trenches." So when I see famous entertainers I don't want to cast myself in the role of "guy who has no business comparing himself to them."

The problem is that I have an uncanny eye for noticing famous people. All their attempts to blend in are lost on me. In the past month alone I've spied: John C. Reily in a boba tea shop, Vincent D'Onofrio in a Starbucks, Magaret Cho walking down the street , Pitbull in an airport in South Africa, Tony Yayo in a diner in Chelsea (nyc), Hassan Johnson (Wee-Bey from the Wire) in the same diner and Leon (Five Heartbeats, Above the Rim, Little Richard story) on the F train in nyc. That's just in the last month!   I could basically be <u>paparazzi without even trying</u>. TMC should install a camera in my goatee.

The problem would be getting sound bites. Not only because my goatee might scratch against the mic but also because I rarely say two words to these people. I try to respect the sanctimony of anonymity.

Cut to me on the F train sitting directly across from Leon. I'm a big fan. He's an amazing actor and also somehow hasn't aged a day in 20 years. I wanted to say hi, not only to compliment his work but also to ask him the secret to his youth (I'm thinking Cocoa Butter must play some kind of role in his daily regimen)

As the F train chugs along, I'm trying to figure out how, when and if I should say something to Leon. I'm also wondering if there's a portrait of him hidden in an attic that maybe has done his aging for him. Just as my brain was approaching meltdown, a guy sat next to

Leon and said, "Hey aren't you Dwayne Perkins?" Huh?

Why yes I am. The guy told me he used to see me perform in LA and was a big fan. I think I spied Leon look the other way with slight indignation as if to say, "What am I chopped liver?" A guy with two names should never upstage a guy with one name. To have only one name, and get away with it, necessarily means you're dope. I felt good but also like a heel. Here is one of the finest actors of our time and I'm getting praised and he's just a guy on the train? No! He's Leon damnit! I was this close to telling the guy who Leon was and trying to transfer the admiration to a more worthy person (If you think I'm cute, you should see my sister).

I never did speak to Leon. As he exited another passenger said, "I think that was Leon?" I was happy that someone on the train said hi to me, maybe Leon would've been happy if I had said hi to him.

Superman Has Left The Building

I recently read about a Chinese dad who makes his 4 year old walk in the snow in his undies to "toughen" him up.

Seeing the boy run through the snow jarred a memory. It brought me back to a time when I found myself locked outside with nothing on but my underoos. My situation was self inflicted. My mom is way too kind and loving to ever take any of her kids through such a harsh regimen. Even if it was "for our own good."

This was way back when a mom could leave a capable child in the house for a few minutes without fear of the feds arresting her or the child drinking paint thinner.   By age 4 don't most kids know that food resides in the fridge or high high above? My mom knew I wouldn't eat anything not fortified with sugar. Taking heed to her explicit instructions not to open the door was another thing altogether.

If I can connect with the 5 year old Dwayne for a minute I think he, me, we wanted a little bit of fresh air. The plan was to open the door fill our lungs with fine Brooklyn sky then go back inside and maybe surf the pre-internet, children encyclopedias. Perhaps I became drunk off my whiff of Brownsville zephyr because I forgot to block the door and it closed behind me. My foray into disobedience was a smashing failure.

I think a neighbor blanketed me until my mom returned. No one thought ill of my mom. And I think a 5 year old boy in Superman underwear is more cute and precocious than anything else.

And that was the day I learned how slam locks really work.

Doppelganger Danger

A few days ago, my sister introduced me to a girl that I went to school with. Except that it wasn't her. It was her identical twin sister, whom I had never met. My sister called her by a different name, so that, of course, threw me for a loop. But... people do change their names (ie Prince became a squiggly, Madonna became Esther, Run became Reverend Run and so on and so on). So in my head I'm like this girl must have an alias. I was scared to say anything on the off chance that she was a spy and blowing her cover would lead to me sleeping with the fishes. But it's hard to imagine my sister mixed up with the world espionage circle. What scared me even more was the possibility that I had forgotten her name. I already do Tae Bo, eat sushi, and buy secondhand clothes. I don't need yet another "Hollywood" label attached to me.

So, I took the leap of faith..sort of. I removed the hood I was wearing (we were outside, nyc) and gave her the crazy presidential cheese smile. Nothing. Then I said "it's Dwayne!" Nothing. Then, I made one last ditch feeble attempt. "Did you go to NY Inst. of Technology?" Eureka!

We were then able to ascertain that she was the twin sister of my old friend.

I'm just glad I didn't know my friend in a biblical way. That could really damage a brother's confidence.

ME: Hey Girl!
HER: Do I know you?
ME: Do you know me?! We spent 9 ½ weeks together back in 99'
HER: Doesn't ring a bell.
ME: Come on?! The pudding? …The bus?… The cops? And what we did to that ferret wasn't even right.
HER: Oh! You're the jackass that caused by sister to get rabies.
ME: My bad. I thought all that foaming of the mouth meant I was putting in work.

MORE TRAVELS

Lights, Camera, Action Heroes

I use long airplane flights to see movies I wouldn't watch in my regular life. If the movie is bad, no skin off my teeth as I didn't pay to see it. If the movie is good, I'm pleasantly surprised and again I didn't pay to see it. An 11 hour flight from Los Angeles to London and another 11 hour flight from London to Johannesburg offers ample opportunity to roll the proverbial movie dice.

So I watched the latest Fast & Furious. They should make another category in the Academy Awards for: Best Action Hero Saying Ridiculous lines while keeping a straight face. It's a gift I tell you. There were easily 10 lines that Vin Diesel said with not a hint of irony that a lesser man could not have pulled off. The badder the script, the better the actor must be to pull it off. Anyone can connect with losing a loved one or a cheating spouse but try telling a bad guy…"You're a bad apple, and tainted fruit salad makes me angry" without giggling. I know I couldn't. They would kick me off the set…

ME: *Can we cut? I'm sorry but who talks like this? See here when I say "Evil doesn't take a day off but I'm gonna make it call in sick." Can't I just say "I'm going to fix the problem"?…okay fine I'll do it your way. I just hope you can edit out my giggling.*

The best at it is Jason Statham. His work in Crank 2 has got to be the best piece of acting ever. He died in Crank 1! He died! So you see everything he does in Crank II is ridiculous. He spends the whole movie trying to get back his heart. But at every step along the way he must recharge the battery powering the fake heart put in by the people who took his real heart out. I'm not sure why they put the fake heart in. They probably regretted that decision 40 minutes into the movie when he came to kick some heart remover ass. Again, I wouldn't last.

ME: *I died in part one! I plummeted to the ground from a hundred stories in the air. Wouldn't that break every bone in my body. Don't your shoes fly off when you fall from that height?*

My friend plays the inquisitive office detective in Fast & Furious. Her job was to set Mr Diesel up for the loaded one liners, saying things like "What makes you so sure?" and "Take a look at this..." She didn't skip a beat and adeptly navigated all the heavy handedness. I sat in amazement at her belief in the utterly unbelievable.

So Jason Statham, Vin Diesel, Clive Owen and all the others who boldly take improbable scripts and execute them like the real pros that they are, I say thank you.

What Happens in the Rest of Vegas…

Living in Los Angeles puts me in close enough proximity to Las Vegas to take an occasional drive out to the city of sin and usually at the urging of a friend. I actually don't love Vegas but I like the drive and it's bearable for a night or two. That's about how long the spectacle of lights, people and shows can distract me from really taking in all the despair that also stays in Vegas. For a night or two I'm in the city the Rat Pack built. After that I'm in the city with slot machines in the super market and cocktail waitresses who should be forced into retirement.

So when I booked a week long gig in Vegas I knew it would be a challenge for me. When I learned that the gig was actually not on the strip but in "Old Vegas" I feared the brushes with sadness might be too much even for me.

Old Vegas is pretty sad. Like a minor league team but literally in the shadows of the big league team up the street. In old Vegas it's much harder to convince yourself that Vegas is anything but a city built on gambling. It's fun and nostalgic, well it could be if the people didn't all look like they escaped from 1987. When you think Vegas, 1950's Frank, Dean and Sammy is nostalgic. 1980's mullets and acid washed jeans are just sad and wrong. I actually had to eat in the employee's cafeteria. An hour in the bowels of any Vegas operation must be like a week in Seattle drizzle.

But nothing trumps the 2 mile area between Old Vegas and New Vegas, aka The Strip of happiness depletion. It's a wasteland of pawn shops and tattoo parlors. You can feel a discernable dip in your endorphin level as you drive through it. It's literally where dreams go to die. I would suggest anyone visiting Vegas to go there first. Get a good visual swig of Rock Bottom before you go into the casinos with delusions of grandeur. Look at all the folks before you who got stuck in the proverbial moat.

That place in between The strip and Old Vegas is like a traffic school video for life. It's like going to a place where everyone has one eye because they didn't listen to their mom when she said "you're going to poke someone's eye out if you keep this up." Imagine how much more heed you would have taken to your dear old mums words if you got a glimpse of all the one-eyed children who didn't listen. Next time you're in Vegas take a gander of the place a little south of the action. But for the love of God man, do so from a moving car.

Can't Judge a Cover By its Book

So I'm on a flight from Jacksonville, FL to Houston, TX on my way, ultimately, to the City of Angels. Which, my trip taught me, could also be called the city of no humidity and no mosquito ambushes. I was actually looking forward to seeing the smog cloud over downtown LA. Well, that and some Witch Hazel and Calamine lotion for nursing the bites obtained in the aforementioned flying bum rush.

There is a descending wish list that most people have in their heads when it comes to who sits next to them on an airplane. For me, No one is 1st, pretty girl 2nd, thin person 3rd and everything after that is a grin and bear it scenario. So as I sat in my window seat, I watched with abated breath as a handful of pretty girls glided down the aisle toward me. Half of which were skinny. Win-win in the airplane row mate game. In life I usually opt for a little more "cushion". But that's neither here nor there.

As I rarely engage my adjacent travelers in conversation, *"skinny eye candy!"* was what I was chanting in my head as the *Who's Next To Me Wheel* spun. My rough estimate of the number of people at the gate made me already accept that "No One" was off the wheel.

Hope turned into disappointment when all the lovely birds walked past my row and my wheel stopped on a 6 foot 5 behemoth with broad shoulders, acid washed jeans and some sort of hybrid mullet under a Budweiser Baseball cap. He was well groomed but that did little to assuage his resemblance to the Geico cavemen. Needless to say I relinquished the arm rest.

The caveman made my jaw drop when he pulled the latest Chelsea Handler book out of his bag and started to read it. *What the…?* Maybe my wish was misinterpreted. Instead of sitting next to a lovely I was sitting next to a guy reading one of the lovely's book. I know Chelsea. She's brilliant, hilarious and very down to earth. I'm just surprised that my formidable friend knew that. Of course, he could have pulled out "Are You There God? It's Me Margaret" and I don't think anyone would give him any flack.

This is the way it should be. People should fight against being herded into a neat little segment that can be marketed to in neat little ways. Remember when people who sell things purport to make things "easier" for you they are probably cutting you off from a whole other world of options you may actually like and benefit from.

I look forward to the day when a Goth girl next to a motor bike rider next to a grandmother all pull out the latest book by Dwayne Perkins and share a little chuckle.

Then I look forward to the day all three pull out the 2nd book by Dwayne Perkins and there's no acknowledgment or surprise. Well, maybe a little surprise that I have a 2nd book out. 😊

Steaks For The Memories

Comedy is tragedy plus time. Sometimes comedy is more instant, like slipping over a banana peel. That's tragedy in an instant. The best comedy is forged in tense, uncomfortable moments and then ready for enjoyment only after the tension has waned and all parties involved are far enough away from the debacle to look back with a jovial tone that almost approaches fondness.

Last night was one for the books. My good friend Jimmy D and I happened to be in Chicago at the same time. We go months without seeing each other in L.A., where we both live, but every time we're in a another city simultaneously, we trip over ourselves to link up. So Jimmy drags his wife out to the outskirts of Chicago to do 7 minutes on my show. The show was a barrel of laughs but only a warm-up for what was to come. Jimmy's a big time foodie. In fact every time I talk to Jimmy, I'm given homework. A new list of all the places where I "must" go and eat. I like food but just point me to a half way decent Thai or Chinese spot and I'm happier than a pig in Pad See Ew.

We're in Chicago, aka foodie Heaven. Jimmy had already texted me pics of places I "just have to try." Obviously I hate being told what to do and I will make a point to never eat at those places. Don't tell Jimmy I said that though. He thoroughly enjoys enlightening me and I thoroughly enjoy ignoring him.

So we're hanging after the show. I'm going to nosh with Jimmy and friends. (kinda sound like the name of a show or maybe a telethon.) Anyhoo, there's no escaping the eatery action item list when you're with Jimmy. Next on his list was Gibson's Steakhouse. I'm pretty sure our way of life as Americans hinged on our small group trekking to this steak house and downing a steak the size of my Ipad.

Gibson's is exactly what you'd imagine a high end steakhouse would be. Solid wood, waiters in sparkling white jackets, even the lighting was setup to subtly let you know that you're about to spend a grip. A waiter came out with slabs of beef on a tray and gave us a well rehearsed spiel on each piece of meat. I feel bad calling him a waiter. He was more of a steak specialist. He went on about the sirloin vs. filet, the rib-eye. He told us they sear the meat on a grill set to 1800 degrees*. The presentation took almost 5 minutes. More homework. After he was done I asked if I could order one of the "demo slabs" he had been touching all night and using for his sales pitch. I figured his fingerprints all over it had to be worth a 50% discount. I also figured 1800 degrees would kill his coodies. He said no one had ever asked that before. I told him it was like buying an opened box TV from Best Buy. He walked away.

He came back and Jimmy and his wife each ordered a steak big enough to feed a village. I ordered a cheeseburger. The table teased me but the waiter assured me the hamburger would be cooked on the very same 1800 degree grill. I also don't like paying more for a steak than I would for a pair of sneakers. The table looked like a clash of spending and eating styles. On one side a vegetarian and a spend thrift, partaking a hamburger and crab meat dip. On the other two all american meat eaters plowing though blocks of all american grade A beef.

I thoroughly enjoyed my burger. It was juicy and tasty and set at a price point that made me not too discerning. I wasn't dropping a car payment so perfection wasn't something I was seeking. Jimmy, however thought his steak didn't live up to its billing. Pun intended. Jimmy's wife wasn't thrilled with her steak either. I told him to complain right away but he forged on and kept eating. He ate his steak like as if it was a puzzle he was taking apart but still needed all the pieces to fit. I think he wanted his steak to look untouched while he continually "touched" it. Like it was magically getting smaller for reasons other than Jimmy's mouth. Jimmy probably was 5 bites beyond the point of an acceptable "send back" of his steak but that didn't deter him. Jimmy called over Alex, the manager guy in a suit who had stopped by to make sure everything was okay a few minutes earlier. He had given us his card. As if our interaction may extend beyond the restaurant. Maybe we would call him with meat inquiries or follow him on twitter to stay current on all things beef. We could retweet his carnivorous quips.

Jimmy explained to Alex that although he had eaten 3/4 of the steak he was very disappointed. Disappointment is apparently uninspired eating over 20 mouthfuls. Maybe because Jimmy had blown past the point of no return or maybe because he wanted to kill an ant with a sledge hammer. Whatever the reason, Jimmy proceeded to qualify himself as a steak connoisseur. Jimmy explained how he's been to all the great steak houses in New York and LA. He mentioned restaurants by name. He mentioned the owners of those restaurants. "I go to Peter Luger's spot all the time. You know Peter Luger?" Jimmy explained that at each establishment he had had the rib-eye. Jimmy's the name and Rib-eye is his game. They use to call him Jimmy Rib-eye back in the old neighborhood. If I didn't know he was talking about steak I would've thought he was speaking on a mob deal gone bad and the guy he was talking to was about to get whacked. "Alex, you broke my heart. You call this succulent?!" Alex responded as if he was about to get whacked and jumped to take care of Jimmy's demands.

It was very uncomfortable but Jimmy stayed the course and made his case and Alex bought out two more behemoth steaks, this time not seared in 1800 degree temps and cooked Medium rare instead of medium plus. Jimmy was pleased. Not sure I could say the same for his digestive track that had basically just been enlisted to process two brontosaurus size tablets of flesh.

The tension was eased when the replacement steaks were delivered. We were all far enough away from the tension to have a good laugh at Jimmy's dropping of steak names. That was a first. Our guffaws reverberated through the steakhouse as the staff waited for us to finish our pecan pie ala mode. (Did I mention they were actually closing at the time Jimmy D filed his complaint?)

Haiku For Jimmy:

Waiting Patiently

While replacement steaks are noshed

Jimmy D eats world

- 1800 degrees fahrenheit is 982 degrees celsius

Thanks again to Gibson's Steakhouse. A real class act.

http://www.gibsonssteakhouse.com/

Check out Jimmy D:

http://funnyjimmy.com/

Operation HAWPO

I want to start a new campaign called (HAWPO) "Help A White Person Out." Here's how it works:

When white people mistakenly say something dumb or that could get uncomfortable, we (minorities) meet them halfway to alleviate the tension. My point is some white people put their foot in their mouths but don't mean any harm. I was recently performing on a cruise ship. It was day three and I hadn't performed yet. An older white couple was behind me on the buffet line. The woman says to me, "We enjoyed your performance last night." Off my look of puzzlement she said, "Aren't you one of the dancers?" HAWPO to the rescue. I said "No, I'm not but I know the guy you're talking about and we do look alike." Tension relieved. I didn't even know the guy. It's not like I could tell one blue-haired couple from the next. I watched the dance show and any one of the dancers could have walked up to me and smacked me in the face and I would not have been able help to cruise ship security one bit in their efforts to hunt down the phantom smacker. "I have no idea who it was but he smacked me, snapped his fingers, did a pirouette, and leaped through the air..."

On the same cruise and in the elevator with several white people. We had all just got back from the port (Puerte Vallarta, Mexico). A white women says to the entire elevator population, "Wow I see we all got burned." Another HAWPO opportunity.

I'm not afraid of confrontation. I'm Brooklyn. I actually thrive on it. I'm just saying battles should be picked wisely and you don't want to fight or alienate someone with good intentions.

Hard to rely on my good intentions....

Kentucky Derby-Less

I just spent a few days in the fine state of Kentucky. Good times. And for all my New York and LA people who think there's nothing to do in other parts of the country…you're right. But there's nothing to do in New York or LA either. When you scale everything down, life is pretty boring. It's supposed to be. Just a humdrum time line with a few spikes of happiness and sadness in their respective directions. And with any luck the high spikes outnumber the low ones. This is true for even the rich and famous. They eat fancier food and sleep on sheets with a higher thread count but when the smoke clears they probably sleep 6-8 hours like you, are in the bathroom 1.3 hours a day*, like you, eat 1.5 hours a day like you and so on and so on… like you. They do vacation in better places…way better places. But what's a vacation except an unfamiliar place to do nothing in.

Strip malls gave me the impetus to say what I just said. **Every** town in America has the same strip mall. A Best Buy, a Bed Bath and Beyond, some discount clothing chain and there's usually a Lowes or Home Depot across the street. And it's is all encased by several Starbucks. This holds true for Los Angeles and New York. LA just has more of these strip malls and New York has them but they're on busy streets and encased by 20

Starbucks and 20 Ray's Original Pizza places(all claiming to be the first)

So what's there to do in Lexington, Kentucky or Kearny, NE…the same more or less that there is to do in New York or LA. Just less lights and not as green salads. I even found an Indian buffet in Lexington.

But if it's some good ole backwards small town thinking you seek…I got some for you. Wearing a helmet while riding a motorcycle is not mandatory in Kentucky. The worst part? It used to be mandatory. What happened Kentucky? Not enough people die? Who championed this cause? Up in arms about preventing head trauma are we?

I'm actually okay with people not wearing helmets or seat belts and long as it means they waive all medical insurance in case of an accident <u>and</u> they get bumped to the end of triage.

NURSE: *Rush the one <u>wearing</u> his seat belt up to the operating room!!…Put the one <u>not wearing</u> a seatbelt in the corner. We'll see him after we take care of Mr. Franklin's hang nail.*

Too morbid of a thought? Surely, not more morbid than reversing a helmet law.

And to all those scooter riders I saw ridings sans

helmet: It's against the spirit of scooter riding to not wear a helmet and you don't look any cooler without a helmet. When you don't have on a helmet you look like your car broke down and you're too broke to fix it and thus are relegated to transport via scooter. When you have your helmet on you seem like a modern day greenster who's decided to save money while saving the environment.

Whether you're a greenster, bad-ass or cruiser, wear a helmet. Your skull will appreciate it.

*if 1.3 hours seems like a long cumulative time to be in the bathroom know that it includes time showering, teeth brushing and saying "you talking to me?!" to the mirror

Out To Pasture

So I ran into an old friend of mine in Kentucky. Actually he's a friend and long time supporter. My friend Michael Blowen used to write for the Boston Globe and during my Boston years he actually gave me quite a bit of ink. And for people born after 1988, no he did not do tattoos for me. He wrote several articles about me, helping both my confidence and my status on the Boston scene.

Turns out he's in Lexington, Kentucky now. From Bean town to Blue Grass..quite a leap indeed. But far bigger than his leap in distance or even culture for that matter is the career leap he made. My friend Michael and his wife now own a horse stable/retirement home. He actually gives former races horses a place to live out their days instead of being prematurely sent to the glue factory. This sounds like the synopsis of a movie or the theme song to a sitcom.

Listen to the Story of a man from the city
traded in his keyboard for a job that's gritty
used to type away, now he bales hay
And spends all his days with the horses that he

saves

(I'm not sure what sitcom melody my diddy goes along with...kinda Beverly Hillbillies but not really...exactly)

The crazy thing is that race horses, even famous ones, are eighty-sixed after their racing/stud days are over. Who knew? They made people millions but aren't even allowed to live out their lives? I mean we do kill cattle but that seems to be the deal from jump. And even that is pretty harsh when you think about it or when you drive by a slaughter house reeking of death and pooh. Admittedly it's a tad more tolerable when you're slamming down a sirloin tip with A1 sauce.

My friend is not only doing heroic work he's also a shining example of how one life can have many chapters. The city boy is now a country boy. Maybe after this he'll open a delicatessen or design parade floats. It's an inspiration to see one of my favorite quotes actually being played out in real life...

It's never too late to be what you could have been.

Old Friends: A Kentucky Facility for Retired

Thoroughbreds

Starbuck Drones

The line in most Airport Starbucks is now officially longer than the security line. I was recently in an airport with two Starbucks in the same terminal within 50 yards from each other. The lines actually met in the middle. All the people waiting in line had to do was hold hands and it would have been a big show of caffeine addicted solidarity across the entire airport terminal. Like hands across the airport terminal*.. I refused to wait. That's the difference between a tea drinker and a coffee drinker. A tea drinker can take it or leave it. They could have spilled all the coffee out unto the floor and charged people 2 dollars for straws. No maintenance clean up would have been needed. It would be a yuppie sip off right in the terminal with "The Girl From Ipanema"** blaring in the background.

Traveler: Johnson! Where are we on the Anderson file? (Sluurrrrp)
Traveler2: (Slurrrrp) everything is good. Just waiting on those 3rd quarter figures.

I'm not sure if Starbucks are franchised but why do drug dealers risk imprisonment instead of selling legal drugs? Sell coffee....they keep coming back too...and you don't have to sell them an espresso behind an abandoned building. Or trade your product for stolen faulty electronic equipment.

"Laughing at baseheads trying to sell some broken amps..." Nas – Illmatic, 1994

*Reference to "Hands Across America" major fundraiser where people joined hands across the entire country. I was one of them. http://en.wikipedia.org/wiki/Hands_Across_America

**Popular Muzak song often heard in airports and supermarkets
http://en.wikipedia.org/wiki/Girl_From_Ipanema

An Affair to Get On My Nerves

I recently had 12 hours to kill on a plane. That last sentence sounded more diabolical than I intended it to. Let me try that again: I was recently on a 12 hour plane ride and decided to watch a few movies to pass the time. There, that's better. One movie being offered in my head rest TV was "An Affair To Remember." This is a classic movie that I, being on the fringe of show business, should have already seen. The movie was cool, perhaps the gold standard for the Romantic Comedy genre. I have to say I enjoyed it, mushy ness and string pulling aside. Well, I enjoyed it until…

ALERT
I'm going to give away the end of the movie in the next paragraph. If you care or if you maybe want to truly **feel** this blog entry, stop reading now, go watch the movie then come back. But since that's a gang of work I'm sure you'll keep reading.
****ALERT OVER****

QSN: *Remember ESPN would show a game on tape delay and give the results to the game being shown on the scroll on the bottom of the screen. Can u say futility? Let the record show…I'm no ESPN!*

So Carey Grant and Deborah Kerr's characters fall in love on a cruise and agree to meet at the top of the Empire State Building in 6 months after they give their respective "squeezes" their respective walking papers. With the one caveat being if they didn't show that would mean they changed their minds or maybe decided to stay in their current relationship. Everything goes as planned except on her way to meet him the girl gets hit by a car. As this movie was set 25 years before even the big backpack cell phones came out she has no way of telling him what happened...Well, that night at least.

So, Carey Grant waits until the Empire State Building closes and leaves thinking he was stood up and the girl decided against being with him. (*Do you think his ears popped on the way down? I'm pretty sure if I was heart broken I might forget to chew gum or hold my nose on the way down.*)

A whole year passes and he doesn't hear a word from her. The accident left her unable to walk, by the way. She doesn't want him to see her in that condition so she would rather he think she just bounced on him. What?! The guy sits around for a year, after breaking off his previous engagement mind you, not knowing what happened. Not one word. And to add 50 scathing "your mother jokes" to injury...Deborah Kerr's character is nursed back to health by her ex fiancé who sticks by her side even though she's in love with Carey Grant...who she won't call. So she has one guy who she loves and who loves her somewhere about to jump off a cliff while a guy who loves her but she doesn't love pays her medical bills and sits by her bed every day just off GP*.

What started out as a good movie had me looking for a

parachute 3 quarters thru (*remember, I was on a plane*). They paint her as heroic but I see it as boundless selfishness. And I don't know who to feel worse for, the guy who she loves or the guy who loves her. I lose interest in any movie the moment the characters do something, for no good reason, that's counter to self preservation.

Of course, in the end the guy she loves miraculously finds her, forgives her, accepts her as is and they live happily every after. The guy who loves her? No one knows. Maybe he fell in love with a woman who lost her sense of taste and ran off to the jungles of Central America for 8 years, leaving no forwarding information, came back despondent having not regained her taste buds but sought refuge in his arms as he welcomed her back with opened arms and vowed to eat bland food for the rest of his life so he could empathize with true love thru all eternity.

I'm not bitter though.

*GP – General Purposes. A hood way of saying for no good reason or just because.

MORE WORLD TRAVELS

That's Entertainment

I had to stop into the Glee Comedy Club in Birmingham, UK on my day off to grab some paperwork. A detail not important to this blog except it's the reason I happened to be there during a Burlesque show. I was coaxed into staying. Admittedly, it did not take Jedi powers to get me to have a sit down.

I thoroughly enjoyed the show. There was truly something for everyone: singing, magic, dancing and poetry. Several thoughts danced across my mind while I watched the performers dance. Not sure if mortality or technical longing is to blame but I wondered if I would remember this night when I'm 90. I stopped taking pictures a few years back because, to quote John Mayer, I wanted to see the world through both my eyes. My picture taking sabbatical is done. It's fine time I hang a rotating picture screen toggling images of places and spaces I've been. Although, I'm not sure what's the policy on taking pics at a burlesque show.

I would have to say that I not only had more fun at the Burlesque show. I also found the women to be more attractive that those of, let's say a strip club. The former probably has a lot to do with not feeling like you're in a dungeon doing something wrong. Strip clubs are like drug dens in that there's an unspoken agreement not to call anyone else out and how could you because you're there too. Burlesque shows pass the mom test. If my mom walked in on me she wouldn't be disappointed that I was there. She might question my affinity for tattoos and Goth but surely she could take in the show with me. Okay, maybe from a different table.

On the attractive front it's easier to enjoy people who are enjoying themselves. I've never been able to go to a strip club and totally look past the glaring misery. The Burlesque girls seem to be having fun and there's at least a real try at entertaining. I'm also already on record as liking some cushion. You never seem to be shorted of that at a Burlesque show.

I was weary of staying at first because Burlesque shows seem so cultish and incestuous. Even the show I watched seemed to have audience members that looked a lot like the performers. Like they were just going to switch places for next week's show. Like a bunch of Paul Reiser's sitting at a Jerry Seinfeld show. With the casual sport coats replaced by lace and red highlights. Being an army of one, I never really feel completely comfortable in culty situations. Watching the show made me realize that what I saw as incestuous was really a judgment free zone.

And that's the beauty and appeal of the modern day burlesque show. It's a fun time where performers and audience members can let themselves go without the need to self edit or worry about who's watching. Kind of like adult kickball but a gazillion times more fun.

By The Dashboard Flight

Dwayne's the name and taking long flights are my game. Nothing like getting in a movie or two, listening to Adele, Vampire Weekend, Kings of Leon, and watching a documentary on the plight of the African bee while you nosh on your in-flight vittles.

Another staple of long flights is the navigation page where you get to see where in the world is your plane. The plane on these maps is always the size of Rhode Island and I spend a considerable amount of time wondering if we're at the nose, the back or in the middle of the map's giant plane.

Enter Air New Zealand with the best navigation page yet. Yes they offer the near life sized plane completely covering Nova Scotia en route to London but they also show a mockup of the plane's dashboard. What? I get to fly this puppy...sort of?! All I needed was a captain's hat and a lollipop to look the part of the 10 year old this neat feature turned me into.

Having the dashboard also makes for great back seat flying.

ME: I can see by the panel that we're straight and level...wait a minute we're dipping. Adding more thrust? Cool I was gonna suggest that actually.... Yes, we're banking left to cut down on wind resistance, my sentiments exactly. Flight attendant, could you please let the captain know that Dwayne in 46G is smelling what he's cooking.

That dashboard probably prevented me from

getting in that forth movie.

A Stone's Throw

They say people in glass houses shouldn't throw stones but I say they can as long as they open a window first. Run your hands over your glass dwelling until you find your window. Your "window" is a small hole in your translucent igloo that makes you different than the person you're about to pelt with judgment pebbles. Perhaps an application of the glass house stone toss exemption is in order.

I was in London recently with a whole lotta of late-nite free time on my hands, a whole lotta stuff to do online and not a whole lotta free wifi. Paying for internet in hotels or cafes went out with barbed-wire arm tattoos. So when you get caught between the moon and London Town with computing needs and little computing options, you may have to head to the only thing open late in London, The Golden Arches. I found a 24 hour McDonald's in Kensington and set up shop. The freaks do come out at night so I had to keep one eye on the screen and one eye on the hungry inebriated clientele. I went to Mickey D's four nights in a row at midnight and stayed until 3am. And every night there was this guy there sitting in the same seat nursing a coffee. I

356

was about to label my fellow fixture a strange loser who hangs out in Mickey D's every single night. I almost hit print on my mental label maker when I realized...

Glass House: ... that I too had been hanging out at Mickey D's every night...

Window: ...Of course, I had work to do and I only went there for the free wifi and to get enough holes punched in my frequent tea card to earn a free tea before my exodus from Jolly Old...

Some windows aren't opened as wide as the thrower would like.

This whole thing took me back to another glass house incident. I was once in a McDonald's in Massachusetts and the person helping me was a little mentally slow but definitely capable of fielding my order. When the man helping me left to assemble my order the cashier at the next register made some disparaging remarks about him being slow and how it was a drag to work with him and blah blah blah.

Glass House: You're teasing someone based on lack of ability but they do the exact same

job you do just as well as you do it. Really?
Aim high.

Window: N/A(There is no window and I hope
she cut herself on a shard of glass)

In a Mess Hall, With His Chest Out

Prison seems to be a voyeur's delight, a place far too brutal to be in but too brutal to not look in on if given a danger free opportunity to do so. I've never really been one for reality shows especially the ones that actually capture reality. I'm not an enjoyer of train wrecks. The only thing I liked about the show "Cops" was the song. By the time they showed a tweeker with his shirt off arguing with his "old lady", I was already watching "Wings."

So my decision to watch a prison show in my hotel room in London was a tad bit ill-advised. I was lured in by the premise: A top notch restaurant in a prison, run by prisoners, caters to civilians. See how different their prison shows are?! The show followed 3 prisoners who wanted to work their way up from the mess hall kitchen to the prison restaurant and hopefully get duly employed upon their release.

One prisoner had the eye of the tiger...

PRISONER1: I'm gonna turn me life around

mate.

PRISONER2: That's what everybody says, mate.

PRISONER1: I'm not everybody. Ya know wha I mean?!

Okay, I'm in. Let's see the wayward blokes filet their way from prison bars to five stars. Only 1 made it. It was the one with the eye of the tiger. The other two seemed to prefer prison, both squandering the opportunity by deliberately breaking prison rules.

It may have done me good to hear people with English accents who are bad asses. It's hard for American ears to hear English accents and feel danger.   The Brooklyn handbook discourages sleeping on anyone at anytime.   I know they're hooligans and we know England has given us multiple heavyweight boxing champs. So they're not to be taken lightly but honestly even the bad asses make me smile when they talk.

I think the show helped me make great strides in respecting English thugs when one prisoner stabbed another in the face. It's all fun and games until someone gets stabbed in the face.

If that doesn't stop my sleeping, nothing will. When you think about it, English bad asses are worse because they get up close and personal with their victims.   If shooting someone is baking a cake, stabbing someone is making that cake from scratch in a wood stove. Anyone can throw egg in a mix and bake it but how many are willing to sweat and toil over an old stove with no recipe and the barest of materials.

This blog didn't set out to be an anti-gun blog but think, how many cakes would you have baked if there was no instant cake mix?

WWE Moment

I was checking email in the lobby of my hotel in Birmingham, England. I was in the lobby because it was the only place free wi-fi was offered. I was watching the WWE^ because that's what was on the television in the lounge where the free wi-fi was. Ta dah!, and there is my airtight excuse for watching junk television. Like when you're in a coffee shop and they're out of bran muffins and only have Danishes left. You wince and sigh as you're "forced" to get a Danish but inside you're dancing and singing "When The Saints Go Marching In." Of course, they'll be marching in with apple Danishes. Who wouldn't want to be in that number?

The WWE was quite amusing. I even found myself laughing out loud.   It's wonderfully comically how the "bad" guy gets away with so much and the referee is somehow always looking the other way and never catches him. But you let the good guy say boo and the ref is right there wagging a finger at him. The best is when the ref is shaking a finger at a good guy while his partner is getting hit with bottles and stabbed by two bad guys in the corner. The crowd is beside themselves and they can't accept or understand why the dumb ref is missing this. Is this ref on loan from the NBA?

I laughed at how predictable it all is, almost to the point of being comforting. This is the same shtick that's been done since I was a kid. I can laugh now but as a kid I would be outraged. My day literally spoiled by an incompetent WWE referee. It's theater in its most primitive enjoyable form. The wrestlers could wear bigger shorts though. I mean really.

As a kid there were a few things that made me want to write my congressman. I seriously wanted to jump in the television when the rabbit was denied his Trix. The day we voted to let him have them was one of my happiest and forever cemented by faith in the democratic process.* I was also driven to hysteria by Batman taking so long to reach his utility belt.

I would like to think my cinematic tolerance has grown proportionately with my age but sadly I can't. I don't do well with suspense and if you see a movie with me that has me on the edge of my seat. Expect to have your arm squeezed 1 second from numbness. I can't take a girl to a horror film because neither one of us would have anyone to turn to.   We would have to bring a third person to calm us both down.

At least I can watch the WWE now without throwing things. I still can't watch Batman take 2 minutes to reach his belt while a saw threatens to cut him in half. And yes I know it's fake but my stomach doesn't seem to.

^ http://www.wwe.com

* http://en.wikipedia.org/wiki/Trix (cereal)

Dubai Series: 1st Installment: Ski At Last

So for my second time in Dubai I just had to partake of one of the things Dubai is famous for. That's right folks I went skiing in the indoor, man-made ski slopes...in the mall! I don't usually advocate this kind of excess. I mainly did it just to say I did.

But what started as whimsy quickly proved to be worth it. I'm a convert. I'm totally in favor of indoor skiing. There's nothing like going to the mall with shorts on, eating an Auntie Annie's pretzel then hitting the slopes. No 5 hour drive, no snow tires, no jacket. Just show up and ski and when you leave its still 85 degrees outside.

I know we're supposed to be going green. Many of you reading this are already green... with envy (I couldn't resist). Don't be hatin'! I guess we have to pick and choose what to environmentally splurge on. I say add indoor skiing to the splurge list. I for one am willing to watch an hour less of TV per week and occasionally carpool if it means I get to Ski, then head over to the Gap for a Jersey knit cotton, super soft T-shirt. I'll just skip "For The Love of Ray J" every week. Are you willing to give up "For the Love of Ray J" for indoor skiing?

At Ski Dubai, you get a jump suit with the price of the ski rental. Ski Dubai even has a little "lodge" at the top of the slope in case you want to grab a hot cocoa and join in on a few sing-a-longs. Skiing is basically going up slow just to go down fast. I don't see why we need to drive hours from home in the freezing cold to engage in that exhilarating monotony. Plus , it's like being in a huge refrigerator and I've always kind of wanted to know what it would feel like to be cold cuts.

Oh yeah, I hadn't skied in over 15 years and I went down the slopes 7 times without wiping out. (That's of course if you don't count the one time I wiped out getting on the ski lift. That shouldn't count right?)

Dubai Series: 2nd Installment: Knock the Man Off Your Polo Sweater

Every time you go to Dubai you're probably going to experience a fair amount of "firsts."My recent trip to Dubai provided me with my 1st polo match.Well, my 1st polo match *viewing*. Although, I was ready to jump in and play as long as they were okay with my new "flat on your belly hand around the horse's neck," riding style.

Here's the kicker…no one in attendance paid any attention to the polo match. It was more like a fashion show and a polo match broke out. Maybe the onlookers were used to the majestic animals going full speed and stopping on a dime then changing direction or the riders hitting a little ball with a stick while galloping at full speed. Or maybe looking cute and sipping libation takes precedence over thrilling action.

I was torn between being mellow like every one else and rooting like I do at Baseball games.

ME: Get glasses Ump, that was legal a bump?!Nice Back Shot!

If I didn't have to perform for the crowd after the game I

may have had more fun with the cheering.

The most excitement came when one of the riders fell off his horse. Everyone watched with abated breath. When he turned out to be okay everyone exhaled a sigh of relief and went back to ignoring the match.

Crazy how all of the people I grew up with who wore Ralph Lauren -Polo Brand clothing like it was a religion will never even sniff an actual polo match…I ignored one.

How was the after show? Well, let's see…an outdoor comedy show for a bunch of tipsy, apathetic people (most of whom spoke English as a 2nd or 3rd language), with a huge fountain separating the comics from the crowd…How do you think it was? It's the kind of show where you just race through your jokes while you picture your paycheck.

Dubai Series: 3rd Installment: Shop Til you Drop Knowledge

I actually visited two different malls on my 4 day stint in Dubai. I felt a bit silly going to the mall. You don't travel across the world to go to a mall. But I needed an adapter for my cell phone. Luckily for me the mall my concierge sent me to doubled as a museum/theme park. You could shop or explore all the countries visited by Arabic explorer Ibn Battuta.

Each section of the mall is named after one of the countries he visited. Each has a motif and food court indicative of their respective countries. Plus there's a huge display dedicated to Ibn Batta. A junior high school girl could go to Forever 21, meet some cute boys and do a book report all in one afternoon. A grandma could put on a powder blue jump suit and seriously get her speed walk on as he strolled through: Andalusia, Tunisia, Egypt, Persia, India, and China.

Shopaholics can site their thirst for knowledge as the reason they have to go to the mall every week.

SHOPAHOLIC: I went there to study... but I had to buy this jacket...it was marked down from 500 Dirhams!

Somehow this huge mall that looks like 6 different countries had four Starbucks. That's 600 Sarah Mclachlan CDs if you're keeping score at home.

When you're in a place that averages temps of 90, trips to the mall begin to make more and more sense. This way you can feel a little more cultured and a little less lame, all while saving on air conditioning costs.

Shout out to Cell Com for having Treo accessories. *(Yes I still have a Treo…well Centro to be exact)*

http://www.ibnbattutamall.com/

Dubai Series: 4th Installment: Ballin!

In between my skiing, mall runs and polo matches I was able to squeeze in some nightlife during my stay in Dubai. My hosts took me to a place called club 360. It was setup like a dark bingo hall with many long tables lined up across the room. Each table came preset with an assortment of beverages, some alcoholic and some not. Basically, to accommodate all the VIPs, it seems they've made the whole club a VIP section. People buy out a table. It makes it easier to get a drink but people just stand around their tables and don't intermingle. It looks like a bunch of people dressed up to play tag and they're all on base and no one is "it."

With everyone balling, of course there has

to be a way for some to ball a wee bit harder. And there was a way my friends. Whenever someone buys a huge bottle of champagne the music comes to a screeching halt and some gladiator type music comes on. Then the bottle, with huge sparklers shooting out from the top, is hoisted through the crowd by some yoked big bottle bearers. Some of the bottles are almost the size of a Russian gymnast. It's a very effective way of letting the whole club know you just dropped over a grand. *Okay, now I know who to ask for spare change.*

Alas, the balling was out of control. Every 5 minutes a different dude, wanting to prove that he too was far from broke, kept preempting the music with a bottle purchase. There were so many bottles with sparklers, I was sure the fire alarm would go off (which I'm told has happened before, BTW).

I wonder if they would have got mad if I had ordered a water and lit my own sparkler.

Different Strokes For Different Blokes

I was on my way to my hotel from London's Heathrow airport. (Right now you're probably thinking I have a great life. You're thinking that because I do ☺ But I digress.)

My driver starts talking politics with me and the other comic in the car, Jasper Red. He's going on about Bush, Blair and the war. The shocker, maybe of the century, was when Condolezza Rice came up. He kept going on and on about how hot she was. At that point Jasper and I look at each other like, "we must be getting punked?!" He not only thought she was pretty but he also thought she had great legs. Someone is really paying attention to those press conferences. Now, I knew I was in a different country but had I also been warped to a new dimension? We told our driver that he would be hard pressed to find an economy car full of Americans that shared his sentiment. He was firm on his Condi is hot position.

He was so sure of himself that I had to re-think the matter. Is Condoleeza Rice hot.

Maybe I've been blinded by what she represents. If Condi came to my hood and gave out gold bricks to everyone, would I think she was a dime piece*? Condi Nice?!?

The driver is from Sri Lanka**. I like to call him no taste Tony. I'm not sure if he speaks for all Sri Lankans but if he does I think we've found the perfect vacation spot for Condi.

*Dime Piece: A perfect ten.

**http://en.wikipedia.org/wiki/Sri_Lanka

Clothes or No Clothes

In the original English version of Deal or No Deal the briefcases are opened by everyday people not scantily clad ridiculously hot chicks like the US version. Why did the US producers feel a need to add this component? I'm not complaining but I think the show has enough suspense without all the skin. I think seeing someone win a million dollars is entertainment enough. This reminds me of guys who say they go to Hooters for the wings. I guess we're still not as bad as Spanish TV. On Spanish TV they'll have a woman reporting from war-torn Iraq in a G string...That's probably why all my views of the war have a Latin slant. 😀

MORE FUNNY, CUZ IT'S TRUE

From Whence I came

I was in Chicago doing shows all last week. Fun times. I was working Zanies, a very classy, hip yet real club, the name notwithstanding. So what did I do after a very fun and fulfilling show at Zanies? That's right I went to an open mic.

A young Chicago comic invited me and I said what the hay. It was pretty brutal, like looking at fashions from the 80's...*Did I really dress like that?* As I watched the comics I kept thinking... *was I that bad?* But I probably was. Watching open mics are like listening to a kid learn how to play Tuba. It's got to be real bad before it can get good. Sure some kids make a pleasant sound sooner than you would expect but only one in a million is a virtuoso out the gate.

I actually went up as my name was *mysteriously* put on the list. I had an okay set but I think my professionalism was a bit of a betrayal. Who's this guy following some sort of convention?! Many open mic comics are done in by trying to make comics in the back of the room laugh. Comics are a cynical jaded bunch and what makes them laugh is often not palpable to common folks. Imagine how spicy food has to be to make a Thai chef sweat. Probably the type of heat that would make a civilian call in sick.

I also couldn't help but wonder who would still be doing comedy 3 years from now and who would be an armchair comic telling their kids how they did comedy a few times one summer back in 09. I know from experience that some of the strongest ones out the gate will lose the fire or be led down a different path. Some of the awful ones might miraculously put it all together and I may be asking if I can open for them one day. You never know but there's something magical about that phase of comedy or anything I imagine. It's not about money yet and at the same time potential and hope creates a promise or at least possibility that they all will make it. No one's been plucked out of the bunch yet so they all have claim to the prize to the crown of best comic ever. Of course time will say different but good bad or worse they're all stars right now.

Piece-O-Cake

I looked in my cupboard the other day and realized that I had a surplus of boxed cake mix. A result of too many 99 cents store runs and not enough festive celebratory dessert bake-offs. There's been stuff to celebrate but I kind of forgot about all that mix collecting dust in my cabinets. So, in the spirit of consolidating, I decided to bake a cake. I basically made a cake because I had too much cake.

MY FRIEND: You're making a cake. What's the

occasion?
ME: Cake, cake is the occasion.

Just after I poured the cake mix into the pans and began to lick the excess batter, I remembered I had a show that night and had to leave in 30 minutes to make it there on time. Exactly the amount of time it would take to cook the cake.

QSN: I'm all about licking cake batter. If you ever sample a Perkins bundt and think it's a hair smaller than a normal bundt, it's probably because I downed more than my share of uncooked cake batter. I know the risks associated with eating raw egg but those are dice I gotsta roll.

I showered while the cake rose and barely had time to take the two layers out of the oven on my way out of the door.

CUT TO:

3 days later when I finally had or made time to frost my cake...

My cakes had settled into their temporary housing and seemed very reluctant to leave the pans and relocate unto a plate. Or to paraphrase: Getting my layers out of the pans was impossible and they both broke in 3 pieces. I put the cake back together like it was a spongy children's jigsaw puzzle. I proceeded to frost the unattached pieces in an attempt to make them one. A cake that's frosted together stays together. Well my cake was dysfunctional and even Dr Phil couldn't fix it. I basically had to dab the cake with frosting because even the slightest spreading caused major breakage. Frosting a crumbling cake is definitely one of the hardest most frustrating things I've ever done and yet in some weird way if was fun. The whole process was too silly to get mad at and luckily my cake didn't have any destination other than my counter and my belly.

In the future, if, I have any impromptu bake-offs I will make sure I have time to remove the pastries and do any of the finishing touches as well.

For Goodness Cake

So my soon to be ex-roommate decided to bake a cake. Don't read into my terminology, the parting is quite amicable. I only use a slightly hostile tone up front because of what follows in this blog.

My roommate is a craftsman at everything he does. He has a natural attention to detail that usually serves him quite well. Every now and then though this attention to detail can slip into "doing too much". Yesterday, he did way too much.

He decided to help with the excess box cake mix inventory by baking a cake of his own. It's cake clearance month down at La casa de Perkins and Smith. Everything must go!! Cool, I'm down with the bake off...The Superbowl, wings, dip and cake. Why not? He does a bang of job of greasing the pan, baking the mix to perfection, I think he through in some vanilla... I really can't hate at this point.

And now we get extra...

So, to spruce up his cake, as if cake really needs any sprucing, he decides to get way creative on the frosting front. First off, he went with white cream cheese frosting. Not what I would have done but hey, it's his cake. Second, he put a layer of chocolate frosting in the middle. Okay, I guess. Third, he put sprinkles on top...But wait it gets worse...forth, he put a layer of peanut butter in the middle as well, hold on, I'm not done...he also packed the middle with marshmallows.

Was he making a cake or a finger painting mural? This is the kind of concoction an 8 year old comes up with when for the first time in his life he's given creative control. His imagination joins forces with his naiveté and his intoxication from having endless choices for the first time ever to create an inedible masterpiece. (Not saying my roommate's cake was inedible just really bad for your health)

QSN: To prove my point warp to an earlier blog I wrote about my best cake experience ever…

http://dwayneperkins.blogspot.com/2008/03/cake-that-took-cake.htmlHalf out of respect and half out of self destructiveness, I tried a piece. It was warm and quite delicious, then the room started to spin. I have never lost my appetite after eating sweets. It's an old adage that I thought had no basis in truth. Well, I ate a slice of the marshmallow death cake at 7pm and did not take another bite of anything for the rest of the night. I basically had to put myself through a mini detox. I was sad from the massive sugar high but I had to be strong and fight through it for my family. I'm proud to say that I've been clean for 12 hours. I'm taking it day by day but I know I can never have yellow cake with cream cheese frosting, peanut butter, chocolate frosting, sprinkles and marshmallows again…ever.

Our ancestors very painstakingly went through millions of cake permutations to give us the cake combinations we have come to accept as good: yellow cake/chocolate frosting. Red velvet cake/White cream cheese frosting... and so on. They did the work for us so we wouldn't have to. I'm sure they tried something similar to the aforementioned cake but stopped making it after the whole village slept for 16 hours straight after eating it.

Bent on Being Like Beckham

I can proudly say that I am not often envious of people. Even in the rare times when I find myself coveting I can usually put the brakes on before I spiral into full playa hatin'. I especially don't envy people's wardrobes. I'm more than okay with my assortment of sneakers (currently anchored by my black Adidas Sambas, Black on White Shell Toes and all white Starbury's). I get no complaints on my track jackets (my East German Army one being the jewel of the bunch). And my blazer T-shirt look pops with hip-hop inspired Teruo shirts underneath.

Pardon the run down of my wardrobe staples. I just wanted to establish that I'm conscious of my attire and for the most part I'm cool with it. I don't see rappers and run out to Macys. R&B singers don't make me doubt myself. Even Athletes don't shake my foundation.

Well, except for one. I find myself catching Beckham on the tellie from time to time and always thinking, "Where did he get that?!" Married men don't usually trump single men in dressing. The married men, for all intents and purposes, are done impressing. Maybe it's the Posh effect but Beckham has some mean threads. And I've never seen him wear anything twice. You can see me rock my East German Army Jacket all over Youtube and even on my CD cover. Heck, I'm wearing it as I type this blog.

So here's what I propose: I want David Beckham to give me his clothes he no longer plans on wearing. I don't want the shirt off his back, just the one in his hamper. I think it's fair time A-listers to pass on their clothes to the E and F-listers. What about the poor Dwayne? I got that covered. I'll give them my clothes. You can't go from shirtless to Beckham's shirt. It's too big of a leap. Going from nothing to so much style may cause internal riffs in the wearer. My clothes will be a manageable step up.

So why am I telling you? Because I want you to help me get this message to Beckham. They say there are only 6 degrees of separation that means I know someone who knows someone who knows someone....

Who knows maybe Beckham already gives his hand me downs to Ryan Seacrest or Mario Lopez*. Well, there's a new boy in town and he's feeling good and wants to look good in Beckham's old clothes.

Seriously though, how many times do you think he wears a given outfit? I say four max. Don't let me down Blog-o-sphere let's get ya boy dressed smart like an English bloke.

*I'm not saying Ryan or Mario are E listers, btw.

King of Wistful Thinking

A few days back I found myself in a melancholy mood. Somehow these moods are often accompanied by me listening to Go West's "King of Wishful Thinking" over and over. I'm not sure if the mood sent me in search of the song or the song puts me in the mood. Probably a little of both.

I was chomping on an apple watching the video on youtube (I guess you could say it was melancholy light, same great "melan" with only half the "choly.") Suddenly my self indulgent state of slight glum was shifted to curiosity. My self-indulgence was broke by an observation…

Guys with receding hairlines used to be allowed on MTV. And not just as the parent of a spoiled 16 year old. They were allowed to be the stars, the front men even. Here was Go West's front man donning a hair recession in a video that was a big hit and surely got VH1 love but probably some MTV "strong like."

Then I thought about all the early MTV acts that were full fledged adults: Dire straits, ZZ

393

Top, Bruce Springsteen, and so on. Of course many of these acts predated MTV and were already stars. So when MTV started they needed to incorporate acts with strong name recognition. Somewhere along the way MTV realized they could manufacture stars in house. Especially since they owned the channels of distribution. We're talking vertical integration here folks.

Also, I think the MTV of yester year predates, but not by much, our absolute worship of youth and the young. We all desire youth and the further away you get from it the closer you get to the grim reaper. (Probably why I'm doing the P90X workout routine ☺) But when I was a teen I had something to look forward to ... and I still do, thank you very much. Now all the youth have to celebrate is youth but even an immortal teen or twenty something knows deep inside that youth is fleeting. I worry about having 22 year olds who think their best days are behind them. At the same time 50 year olds are trying to wear skinny jeans. Funny it seems we're extending youth and condensing it all at the same time.

MTV: please let guys with receding hairlines back on your network. Maybe they won't feel the need to tuck their jeans into their high top

Nikes if you do.

A Very Special Golden Girls

At some point even your silliest sitcoms will throw out a Very Special Episode (VSE) for your viewing un-pleasure. The "Very Special" episode usually deals with a subject way too heavy to be dealt with in a 22 minute comedy.

QSN: Who can forget the Different Stroke episode when Dudley got molested.* Two boys from Harlem falling for the Okey Doke? Unlikely. Different Strokes probably had the most VSEs. When you think about it the very premise of that show hovered around being "Very Special."

I'm watching Golden Girls on Lifetime last night and I guess I forgot that the good ole Golden Girls threw a big hat into the Very Special mix. The viewer had to wait the entire episode to find out if Rose was HIV+ from a possibly tainted blood transfusion. That's too much stress for a Golden Girls episode. Isn't it traumatic enough that on any given episode one of their friends might die? They did ask the obvious question though: Why Rose and not usually horizontal Blanche. The lesson? Bad things happen to good people? Older people need to be safe as well?

The only lesson I learned was to make sure I travel with my nail clippers, because I spent the entire episode biting my nails. In the end Rose did not have HIV. That's the only thing we can really learn from VSEs. The lead characters always escape any horrible fate, unless they're in a contract dispute with the producers. See James Evans on Good Times** or Valerie on Valerie. (NBC fired "Valerie", killed her character and renamed the show The Hogan Family. Now that's hardcore!) ***

Two sitcoms never had VSE's. The two best ever. Seinfeld, because they had a strict no growth, no lessons policy and All in the Family because they tackled issues on every show so no one show was glaringly poignant for no good reason.

* here's the Different Strokes episode. Very uncomfortable. Very funny http://www.youtube.com/watch?v=Tm535nFNZlo

**Damn, Damn,Damn Good Times info http://en.wikipedia.org/wiki/Good_Times
***Valerie info: http://en.wikipedia.org/wiki/Valerie_(TV_series)

Wedding Scrum

The priest at a wedding will always say the purpose of the ceremony is for the couple to make their vows in public. In essence they're making a promise to friends and family as well. I get that. I also get that for the couple's loved ones the ceremony is a celebration slash official "handing over" of both bride and groom. I say the wedding ceremony is done to remind and encourage people about the virtues of holy matrimony. The wedding is marriage's big day to recruit new members and to rejuvenate those already hitched.

Most comedians and sitcoms focus on the daily grind that is marriage. For the most part marriage is painted in a so-so light. For someone choosing, it's hard for stability to look more appealing than adventure and even those with stability seem to crave spontaneity. So this institution, although healthy for the human soul, is a long long haul and thus needs a tremendous send off party. And it needs to be majestic to reverse, in one afternoon, all the notions of marriage fed to us on a daily basis. A tall order but the concept of love is powerful. Thus nearly every wedding I have attended made love and the union of love seem not only good and necessary but also intoxicating and inspirational.

I say all that to say this, Let's eliminate the bouquet toss! The whole thing completely derails the romance train. It's like you're on a train from Paris to Cannes with breath taking scenary but then you somehow stop in Barstow, CA for a few minutes. It's jarring I tell ya. The wedding is a beacon of love and hope in all its splendor while the bouquet/garter belt toss is a microcosm of actual dating in the real world. A score of women tussle like they're in a Rugby scrum to get an unproven promissary note that their big day will be next. Then, a handful of guys reluctantly stand around and make absolutely no effort to catch the garter belt that would suggest they might be next. I have been to six weddings where the garter belt literally hit the floor and the guy nearest to it had to begrudgingly pick it up like a late night shift in a canning factory.

I recently went to a wedding where the bride had caught the bouquet at the wedding where she met the groom. It works! A ready made Hollywood tale. This fact also raised the bouquet stakes. The increase in the collective belief in the power of the bouquet took a little air out of the room and left a vacuum filled with tension and competitveness. One girl dove for the bouquet like it was the superbowl and the ball was fumbled on the one yard line. (an analogy that speaks volumes to the male value system 😀 So basically, the next woman to get married is the one with the best linebacker skills? We're also leaving the whole thing in jeopardy of the "fix". That's when the bride basically lobs it to a friend.

If the wedding ceremony absolutely needs a "to be continued" compenent, let's make it truly random and computerize it. That way, no single men can sit out the garter belt toss and women don't have to choose between being a spinster or a competitor in a high heeled mosh pit.

The wedding is like a first kiss. The bouquet toss is realizing the other person has their eyes open. So adios to the toss and if we could not do the cha-cha dance that would be much appreciated as well.

God Bless You and Your Mouth

I recently had surgery to repair a hernia. I didn't know light circuit training could do that. It was my first time under the knife and under anesthesia. The anesthesiologist told me he was giving me just a little to make me feel better but not totally put me out, as I wanted to talk with the doctor before he gave me the old slice and dice. That's the last thing I remembered. They told me to tell my ride to come get me at noon. A hernia operation is day surgery and I was the first one in. In fact, I woke the rooster up on my way to the surgery. I didn't wake up until 2pm in all types of pain and nauseous from the anesthesia. It wasn't until 4pm that I mustered up the courage to try and leave. Some guy in the room next to me had hernia surgery and he just walked out afterwards. He probably went dancing that night. I, after asking if I could stay overnight and getting shut down quicker than a Korean restaurant at closing time, had to be wheeled out. I tried eating bread and just spit it out right on the hospital floor like a stubborn one year old.

I eventually got better. After about a week, I was walking okay, and out of the blue, I sneezed. I can't really describe the pain, but I'll say a sneeze is a very violent action that you never think of that way until something is hurting. Someone could have taken me hostage with a pepper shaker. If I had sneezed the day of my surgery, I'm not sure if I would be writing this blog right now. Even after a week, every sneeze was followed with a loud curse. So "God bless you" took on a whole different meaning. Don't go to church when your healing from Hernia surgery and have the sniffles.

BTW: A hernia is a hole in your abdominal wall.

The Snow Must Go On

I recently had 2 shows in two nights in Michigan and had to drive from one to the other. The 2nd show was a three hour drive away. So I basically had all day to casually go about my business and take a leisurely drive to the 2nd venue with plenty of time to spare. Enter the snow storm.

Now this storm may be business as usual for the Michiganites but for a person living in Los Angeles and completely out of "practice" it was harrowing. There was a few times when I thought of saying my Last Will & Testament into the voice memo on my phone.

DWAYNE: To my mother I leave the rights to my blog and my T-shirt collection.

Picture, if you will, driving in blizzardie conditions with maybe ¼ mile of visibility with only one lane that's kind of plowed because the cars ahead of you kind of left a groove for your tires to kind of drive in. Now picture, if you will, doing that alone in a rental car, in a place you've never driven and only 1 day before you were cruising in 70 degree weather. I find in these types of conditions most drivers fall into 2 different but equally dangerous categories. There's the guy who doesn't respect or understand reduced friction. He's flying past you in the snow lane like you're the idiot. And as he does he causes snow and debris to envelope your car rendering you blind for a few seconds and now you have to use "The Force" because some A-hole forgot everything they taught him in defensive driving. Almost as bad as Mr. Cavalier though is Mr. 1 mile Per Hour. He's going slower than if he just walked. Go slower but...go! Mr. 1 Mile Per Hour forces me, Mr. Safely Reducing His Speed to become Mr. Cavalier. Albeit for a few seconds so I can pass him. All things are relative.

The 3 hour drive took about 6 hours. I spied 7

wrecks along the way. Cars in ditches some trapped in the breakdown lane facing the wrong way. Some nestled up against a tree. Some cars crushed together like a fallen Transformer. Luckily I had satellite radio in my Sebring and I blasted Old Skool Hip Hop the whole way. If I was going to go out, at least it would be with Kurtis Blow and Dana Dane holding me down. The scariest part of my ride was when I passed one of the "plow" trucks. I use quotes because somehow these monstrosities blow more snow into the air then they clear. Maybe the guy had his settings in reverse. All I know is there was a 30 second interval when I couldn't see a thing. Not even the hood of the car I was driving. I just went slow and prayed the road stayed straight. I finally passed the truck a changed man with a bit of my innocence lost. In the map of my life that time will only have 1 set of car tracks. That will be the time when God towed me. Shout out to Bob & Tom, East Lansing, Manistee and Chrysler.

QSN: This pic was from the day after the storm on my way to the airport.

Tastes Like Chicken

I pride myself on being a pretty accurate guy. A person should only embellish when telling a funny story or when on stage, and even then with care and selectiveness. I think one should always be as accurate as possible. My reasoning is hard to put in words but I feel that unnecessary exaggeration necessarily diminishes the perpetrator's power, life force and ability. A person who exaggerates incessantly may be discontent with their actual life and run the risk of becoming addicted to making up stories to feel adequate. They also run the risk of adopting a victim mentality if their exaggerations tends to stray to the negative.

EXAGGERATOR: My car literally breaks down every other day.
ME: Really? And how long have you had this car? Two years. So your car has broken down 365 times? That doesn't seem reliable. Maybe you should consider taking the bus.

QSN: Ever notice how people who exaggerate use the word "literally" way more than everyone else? If you use the word "literally" more than 10 times a week...cut it out!

And now comes the silliness:

Much like MJ, I'm starting with the man in the mirror. I'm fairly accurate but I do find myself grossly exaggerating on one specific point...

I'm quick to say that something that tastes bad tastes like dog pooh. Having never tasted dog pooh, I'm completely unqualified to make such a declaration. And even if I was qualified, in the name of accuracy, I couldn't stamp the dog pooh label on two completely different dishes; unless of course, I also stated the breed of dog pooh. With my luck I would have a friend nearby who loves accuracy even more than me and is keeping a list of what foods I've linked to what breeds.

ME: This bologna sandwich tastes like Australian Bulldog pooh.

FRIEND: You said that quesadilla tasted like Australian Bulldog pooh last week.

ME: No, I said that quesadilla tasted like Black Russian Terrier pooh...You know...Maybe we should start going to better restaurants.

Twitter Quitter

So I needed to find the hours of a local credit union so I could deposit some sweet sweet cash. (Actually not cash but sweet sweet check doesn't have the same ring.)I went to one credit union's website and Lo And behold they have a twitter account…Huh?

We're talking a bank people! What 140 character information chunks do they need to dispatch all throughout the day? Isn't a bank being on twitter the beginning of the end? Could twitter become lame smack dab in the middle of its burgeoning coolness?

Well, you can keep your Ashton Kutcher, I'm following the Telesis Credit Union.

At 1:31pm they twittered:

We're working on our new Rewards program…more details coming soon!

Thank God they got **that** information out. Seems to me twittering is like reverse stalking. For years it was bad to stalk. We even convicted those we caught doing it and now we basically invite everyone to stalk us. Lift the restraining orders…

STALKER:*If she had a twitter account I would never have bought those binoculars… I just wanted to know what she was eating and doing every hour or so…*

I have not thrown my hat into the Twitter mix*. I would like to say that I won't ever join Twitter but I'll probably fold at some point and be compelled to let the world know I'm in a donut shop eating a Turkey sandwich and washing it down with a milk tea Boba or using my perfect push-ups bars while watching Judge Mathis.

Twitter asks, "What are you doing"? Answer: Not a damn thing but reporting what I'm doing…or should I say **not** doing. Twitter is like organized group Terrets. Stalking is the new black.

*QSN: I've decided to throw my metaphoric hat into the mix. I've folded, my Twitter account is @funnydp. Feel free to digitally stalk me. www.twitter.com/funnydp

Want real excitement?Check out the Telesis Credit Union's Twitter account.

http://twitter.com/TelesisCU

The Bank With a Heart of Gold

Remarkably, someone at Telesis Bank read my recent blog about their Twitter account (Twitter Quitter) and responded to me! How's that for customer service. He wasn't even a tad bit upset at my subtle dig at them for having a Twitter account. He was upbeat and courteous. In all seriousness a Credit Union probably has more to Twitter about than a party girl from Orange County or even Flavor Flav for that matter.

Flavor's latest Twitter...(as I imagine it) Just looked at my chest and guess what...I still know what time it is boyeeee. Why won't Chuck D return my calls?

Even when I wrote the blog I felt the credit union's twitter was more useful than I imagined. First off, to say that would not have been funny and Secondly, I still think that useful information doesn't necessarily need to be delivered at break neck speeds in 140 character chunks.

Here's Brian from Telesis Credit union's response to my blog*:
Thanks for your shout-out to our exciting

411

Twitter site! While we can't take sole credit for upping the lameness quotient on Twitter, we're glad to do our part! 😊

Seriously, though, we hope that using Twitter occasionally gives us a chance to have a different sort of conversation with our members. Remains to be seen if they want to have that conversation, too!

Brian Siegel
Telesis Community Credit Union
www.telesiscu.com
http://twitter.com/TelesisCU

Telesis sees all my friends. I recently contacted some other banks for a sizeable loan that I more than qualify for. I could barely get them on the phone and they would be making a lot of money off me over the long run. I drop a blog about Telesis and not two days later I get a detailed friendly response. They took the time out to write back to me, a G-Lister. I should start banking with them or at the very least hire them to be my publicist.

I got nothing but love for you Telesis Credit Union....You too Brian.

*Comment was posted on my blogger site

hot chocolate for the mind - FINAL

Dwayneperkins.blogspot.com

Off Da Hook

I was recently at a fellow comic's house. I consider him a peer. A peer with 2 kids in High School. He's older than me and maybe he started young but still a peer with children looking at colleges can make a guy feel long in the tooth. These thoughts were not really at the forefront of my mental though. They were more like a program running silently in the background.

Then something happened that made the "The feeling old" app run in the foreground. and close all the other apps running in my head. My friend's daughter made a phone call on her cell. I guess she was calling a home line that was busy. She turned to her dad and said

DAUGHTER: Dad, there's like a buzzing sound.

FATHER: Let me hear it. Oh that's a busy signal. It's what you get when someone is at home and on the phone and they don't have call waiting.

She had lived 14 years and never once heard a busy signal! She probably thinks Bon Jovi is an actor, Mark McGrath is a game show host and Charles Barkley is a sports commentator who gets away with more than most commentators do.

After feeling old for the next few hours I thought of the implications of never hearing a busy signal. It means never waiting. I know I'm dangerously close to saying.."In my day..." From a technology standpoint I realize I had it easy growing up but I actually heard someone in a commercial say "That was so 27 seconds ago"

Is there a point where convenience becomes debilitating? A point where we eliminate work at the expense of eliminating coping skills? I won't say "in my day...." but I will say we are dangerously close to that point of uselessness. How many times have you stayed on the channel you were watching because you couldn't find the remote? Completely forgetting that pressing the buttons on the TV or cable box was an option.

I'm old enough to know what a busy signal is but I'm also old enough to call back or to write and send a letter in the mail and to look up things in a phonebook if needed. It's not exactly living off the land but yes, I am stronger than most kids today. 🙂 Am I'm up on the times as well. I don't even own a home phone, so there.

Get 'er Done...Incrementally

Today, a friend sent me an article about a calendar system that Jerry Seinfeld used or perhaps uses to write jokes and was kind enough to share with other comics. It was sent to me because it reminded my friend of my intricate weekly activity system I have shared with her and anyone else who will listen; a system that I will share with you, my readers, in due time.

Of course, knowing that Mr. "Didja Ever Notice" has a system in any way similar to mine warms my cockles. But for real inspiration I didn't have to look that far. My friend Randall may or may not have an elaborate work system but he does get an incredibly large amount of stuff done. All the work I have done with Randall usually starts with a list being made, items assigned, and then that list getting done. Randall makes a list quicker than anyone I know. And when you pull back and take a wide look it's not hard to see that Seinfeld's system is really just a list, my can't lose system, called "The Grid" among me and my friends, is really just a series of lists.

I think it's fair to say that civilization on a

whole has been built on the making and completing of lists. The Golden Gate Bridge is really the culmination of hundreds of linking lists each with items that were completed until finally a car could drive from San Francisco to Marin.

I don't think anything I've done is as intricate as the building of the Golden Gate Bridge. And, while I do rely on people, there isn't a team of a thousand people who all must do their job perfectly or else I'm floating in the Golden Gate. No, I am the creator and overseer of my list. Sometimes my list will involve working with others or an item on my list will be an item of a friends list. Or an item on my list can be broken down into another list I make with a friend on a side project.

So the question to ask yourself is what is on your list? Will the things on your list, upon completion, build a bridge that you want to cross? Are there things not on your list that should be there? Is there anything on your list not done with no signs of getting done? If so why? There are thousands of publications that promise to help you unlock your power and such. All of them in one way or another will tell you to make a list.

Jerry Seinfeld's Productivity on Steroids

Beautiful Mad Men

"The truth will set you free", is one of those great adages that is always powerful albeit trite. The problem with that statement is that the truth is often hard to see and nothing camouflages the truth like good looks. Good looking people get away with much more than the aesthetically average. (It's a small miracle than I'm not an absolute terror.) If you're beautiful and rich, you can nearly be a psychopath before people will check you.

I love the show "Mad Men." The fact that my friends and I discuss the virtues of the characters like they're real people is a testament to how great a show it is. The main guy, Don Draper is a wonderfully flawed character. That's the consensus at least. Which is what you say about a good looking person who treats others badly. They're flawed but you have to put a positive adjective in front of the word flawed. You can also call them complicated. Be broke and ugly and you're just a dick. Your poor uncle is crazy. Your rich uncle is eccentric.

I suppose the beautiful people got it honest.

Their personalities are forged over a lifetime of being treated better and being held less accountable. Like the ocean gradually turning rocks into sand, pretty people's beach of entitlement is formed by never ending waves of compliments and unearned good will.

On screen we put up with bad behavior because, well they're not real but also they look good so we identify with them. We dream of a world where we have a permanent "get out of jail free card." I guess cutting a fictional character some slack is okay. In real life though, it's the stuff that sociopaths are made of.

We also do pretty people a disservice because when you're told you're great and you haven't attained any modicum of greatness it usually ensures that you'll never reach true greatness. Encouragement is good but propping up mediocrity isn't. This is why good looking people, present company excluded, aren't usually funny. People laugh at their unfunny jokes and so they never get around to telling actual funny jokes.

In the end, I'm not sure if pretty people need our compassion or our tough love. What would you think of Don Draper if he wasn't good looking?

Ain't No Stopping Us Now

I was at a family outing in the Farragut projects in Brooklyn NY. I spent many summer days there in my youth hanging with my cousin and committing misdemeanors. My aunt Debbie cooked up the Perfect Storm. Nostalgia approached dangerous levels as child hood memories rushed back with a flash when I entered the lobby of my aunt's building.

QSN: a quarter of the mailboxes had no doors. Don't people in the hood have it bad enough? Now they have to get PO boxes!

I was in the middle of fixing myself a plate when the song "Aint No Stopping Us Now" came on. That's my favorite song of all time and, judging from my family's reaction, it must be high up on their list too. Everyone reported to the dance floor like a gang of Death Eaters reporting to the Dark Lord.* I ran to the dance floor with a full plate in hand. Dancing there with my mom and other family members, may have been the best 5 minute span I've experienced all year. That song harks back to a simpler time for black folks. It was 79 maybe 80. Crack wasn't big yet. No one had heard of Freeway Rick Ross.** No one knew what a contra was. Reagan wasn't in yet. It was the beginning of a new decade. We had so much hope. Hip-Hop had just dropped.

My uncle Orlando cried tears of joy after the song ended. I'm sure the 5 beers he had prior to the song playing helped stunt his emotional threshold. When asked why he was crying he simply said.

ORLANDO: Family! Family! This is generations!

I felt it too. I didn't cry because I don't cry.*** That song was supposed to symbolize our springboard into our new place in this country but 25 years later and we see that hope just now coming off life support. Orlando's tears of joy were probably mixed with sorrow. What happened to family, to the no stopping us mantra? Drugs and violence sent our dreams spiraling. We lost so many, so many will never be the same. If crack never hit, what would that song mean today? Maybe it would be a historic battle cry instead of an old school jam whose promise was never fulfilled. Or maybe songs like that got us through the rough patches like the footprints poem.

Uncle Orlando, you cry my tears.

BTW: I danced with a full plate in hand without dropping any of my food. That's how I do!

* Harry Potter reference. Voldemort: Harry's nemesis and the source of Harry'scar. Death Eaters: Voldemorts followers who jump to it when old Volde beckons.

** It's been strongly suggested that the CIA had an involvement with flooding our streets with Cocaine in order to fund Nicaraguan rebels during the cold war. Freeway Rick Ross was the LA drug dealer chosen as the main connect. He got cheap drugs from Oscar Danilo Blandon and supplied oodles of LA dealers with the product that flooded US cities and spawned an epidemic of addiction and violence while funding the rebels in Nicaragua. The CIA denies any involvement. John Kerry says otherwise. Personally I believe the CIA had a hand in it but as no one puts a gun to person's head and makes them take drugs, I won't say the CIA is responsible just that they helped proliferate the epidemic. Check the links and Youtube piece and judge for yourself.

http://www.youtube.com/watch?v=FYgwIBXMNho&eurl=
http://en.wikipedia.org/wiki/Ricky_Ross

%28drug_trafficker%29
http://en.wikipedia.org/wiki/
Oscar_Danilo_Blandon

***I cried at the end of Cooley High but hey who didn't. I also may have shed one single tear when I first saw ET and I welled up during Seven Years in Tibet...don't ask.

About The Author

Dwayne Perkins is a nationally, and internationally touring stand–up comic currently residing in Los Angeles. Dwayne was born and raised in Brooklyn, New York and still frequents New York City. He is a regular on the Conan show and was a correspondent on the Jay Leno show where he wrote and performed a segment called "Great White Moments in Black History."

www.averyfunnyblog.com
www.dwayneperkins.com

Final Thoughts:

I would be honored if you would review my book and share it with your friends and family.
Kindle Readers will give you a chance to rate and share this book on your Twitter and Facebook page on the 'Before You Go Page'.

If you're reading on a Kindle app on another device you can go to my book's amazon page to review and share.
http://www.amazon.com/dp/B00ATCKEFK

Thanks for your support
Cheers,
Dwayne Perkins

Acknowledgments

I stand on the shoulders of so many. If I mentioned everyone, this section would be longer than the book. Thanks to every comic to ever grace the stage and especially to those who went on to become writers. Thanks to my Agent Mark Scroggs and everyone at David Shapira and Associates. Thanks to my manager, Matt Schuler for being the man who executes the plan. Thanks to my commercial agents over at Brady Brannon and Rich for getting me in on so many auditions where I didn't even match the breakdown. Thanks to 'Me' and Deana for your faithful readership and support. Thanks to Deana for helping with the monumental task of editing and thanks to Christy Murphy for guiding me through the process.

Thanks to my family for supporting me and

being patient with me throughout my entire career.

Made in United States
Orlando, FL
04 April 2022

16468587R00235